Editorial Project Manager
Eric Migliaccio

Editor in Chief
Karen J. Goldfluss, M.S. Ed.

Cover Artist
Sarah Kim

Illustrator
Clint McKnight

Art Coordinator
Renée Mc Elwee

Imaging
Ariyanna Simien
James Edward Grace

Publisher
Mary D. Smith, M.S. Ed.

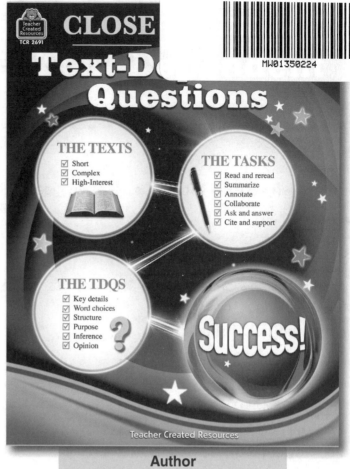

Author
Ruth Foster, M.Ed.

For the Lexile measures of the reading passages included in this book, visit www.teachercreated.com and click on the Lexile Measures button located on this resource's product page.

For correlations to the Common Core State Standards, see pages 95–96 of this book or visit http://www.teachercreated.com/standards.

The classroom teacher may reproduce the materials in this book and/or CD for use in a single classroom only. The reproduction of any part of this book and/or CD for other classrooms or for an entire school or school system is strictly prohibited. No part of this publication may be transmitted or recorded in any form without written permission from the publisher with the exception of electronic material, which may be stored on the purchaser's computer only.

Teacher Created Resources
12621 Western Avenue
Garden Grove, CA 92841
www.teachercreated.com

ISBN: 978-1-4206-2691-9

©2017 Teacher Created Resources
Made in U.S.A.

Table of Contents

Overview 3
    What Is Close Reading? — What Are Text-Dependent Questions? — How Is This Guide Organized?

A Closer Look 4
    The Texts — The Tasks — The TDQs (Text-Dependent Questions)

All About Annotation 6
    Teacher Instruction — Student Sample

Section I Units
Each unit in this section includes a Close-Reading Passage, a page of Close-Reading Tasks, and two pages of Text-Dependent Questions.

    Unit 1: "Dead-Tree Wishes" 8
    Unit 2: "Going, Going, Gone!" 12
    Unit 3: "Helping Hands" 16
    Unit 4: "Biscuit Drop" 20
    Unit 5: "Animal Facts" 24
    Unit 6: "Edward Lear" 28
    Unit 7: "Horribly Sick" 32
    Unit 8: "Crocodile Tears" 36
    Unit 9: "Magic Trick" 40
    Unit 10: "Alive and Dead" 44
    Unit 11: "A Bare Escape" 48
    Unit 12: "The Ins and Outs of Doors" 52
    Unit 13: "Shooting Fish" 56
    Unit 14: "Carrie the Carrier" 60
    Unit 15: "Never Growing Old" 64
    Unit 16: "Always First" 68
    Unit 17: "Sportsmanship" 72
    Unit 18: "On the Leash" 76
    Unit 19: "Surviving the Fire" 80
    Unit 20: "Cat for Dessert" 84

Section II Units
Each unit in this section includes a Close-Reading Passage and a page of Peer-Led Tasks.

    Unit 21: "The Mouse and the Tornado" 88
    Unit 22: "Around the Cape" 90

Answer Key 92

Meeting Standards 95

Overview

What Is Close Reading?

Close reading is thoughtful, critical analysis of a text. Close-reading instruction gives your students guided practice in approaching, understanding, and, ultimately, mastering complex texts. This type of instruction builds positive reading habits and allows students to successfully integrate their prior experiences and background knowledge with the unfamiliar text they are encountering.

There are certain factors that differentiate close-reading instruction from other types of reading instruction. These factors include the types of **texts** used for instruction, the **tasks** students are asked to perform, and the **questions** they are expected to answer. For detailed information on these factors, see "A Closer Look" on pages 4–5.

What Are Text-Dependent Questions?

Text-dependent questions (TDQs) can only be answered by referring explicitly back to the text. They are designed to deepen the reader's understanding of the text, and they require students to answer in such a way that higher-level thinking is demonstrated. To be most effective, TDQs should address all that a reading passage has to offer; the questions asked should prompt students to consider the meaning, purpose, structure, and craft contained within the text.

How Is This Guide Organized?

The units in *Close Reading with Text-Dependent Questions* are divided into two sections. Each of the twenty **Section I Units** (pages 8–87) is a four-page unit.

Page 1 Close-Reading Passage	This page contains a short, complex, high-interest reading passage. Parts of the passage are numbered for easy reference, and space for annotation is provided in the left margin and between lines of text.
Page 2 Close-Reading Tasks	Students are guided to read the passage, summarize it, reread and annotate it, and meet with a partner to discuss and define the author's word choices.
Page 3 Text-Dependent Questions	Students are asked to display a general understanding of the text, locate key details within it, cite evidence, and begin to use tools such as inference.
Page 4 More TDQs	Students examine the structure of the text and the author's purpose. They form opinions and use evidence to support and defend claims. A research prompt encourages choice, exploration, and cross-curricular connections. (**Note:** Monitor students' Internet research for content appropriateness.)

Each of the two **Section II Units** (pages 88–91) contains two pages.

Page 1 Close-Reading Passage	This page contains a short, complex, high-interest reading passage. Parts of the passage are numbered for easy reference, and space for annotation is provided in the left margin and between lines of text.
Page 2 Peer-Led Tasks	This page guides groups of students through a series of peer-led tasks in which each member is assigned a different role. Students become teachers to one another as they work together to analyze a text.

A Closer Look

Close Reading with Text-Dependent Questions focuses on the three main components of close-reading instruction: the **texts** students are asked to read, the **tasks** they are instructed to perform, and the **text-dependent questions (TDQs)** they are expected to answer thoughtfully and accurately.

The Texts

- ✓ short
- ✓ complex
- ✓ high-interest
- ✓ multi-genre

Not all texts are appropriate for close-reading instruction. Passages need to be written in a manner that invites analysis and at a level that requires slow, careful, deliberate reading. The texts in this guide achieve these goals in a number of ways.

- **Length:** Close-reading passages should be relatively short because the rigorous work required of students could make longer passages overwhelming.

Each unit in this guide contains a one-page passage of about 300–325 words. This is an ideal length to introduce and explore a subject, while allowing students of this age to conduct an in-depth examination of its content and purpose.

- **Complexity:** The best way to foster close reading of informational or fictional text is through text complexity. Writing achieves a high level of text complexity when it fulfills certain factors. The **purpose** of the text is implicit or hidden in some way, and the **structure** of the text is complex and/or unconventional. The **demands** of the text ask students to use life experiences, cultural awareness, and content knowledge to supplement their understanding. The **language** of the text incorporates domain-specific, figurative, ironic, ambiguous, or otherwise unfamiliar vocabulary.

The passages in this guide contain all of these different types of language and ask students to decipher their meanings in the context of the parts (words, phrases, sentences, etc.) around them. The passages meet the purpose and structure criteria by delaying key information, defying reader expectations, and/or including unexpected outcomes — elements that challenge students to follow the development of ideas along the course of the text. Students must combine their prior knowledge with the information given in order to form and support an opinion.

- **Interest:** Since close reading requires multiple readings, it is vital that the topics covered and style employed be interesting and varied. The passages in this resource will guide your students down such high-interest avenues as adventure, invention, discovery, and oddity. These texts are written with humor and wonder, and they strive to impart the thrill of learning.

- **Text Types and Genres:** It is important to give students experience with the close reading of a wide variety of texts. The passages in this guide are an equal mix of fiction and nonfiction; and they include examples and/or combinations of the following forms, text types, and genres: drama, poetry, descriptive, narrative, expository, and argumentative.

- **Lexile-Leveled:** A Lexile measure is a quantitative tool designed to represent the complexity of a text. The passages featured in this resource have been Lexile-leveled to ensure their appropriateness for this grade level. For more information, visit this resource's product page at *www.teachercreated.com*.

A Closer Look (cont.)

The Tasks

- ✓ read and reread
- ✓ summarize
- ✓ annotate
- ✓ collaborate
- ✓ connect
- ✓ illustrate
- ✓ cite and support
- ✓ ask and answer

An essential way in which close-reading instruction differs from other practices can be seen in the tasks students are asked to perform. This resource focuses on the following student tasks:

- **Read and Reread:** First and foremost, close reading requires multiple readings of the text. This fosters a deeper understanding as the knowledge gained with each successive reading builds upon the previous readings. To keep students engaged, the tasks associated with each reading should vary. When students are asked to reread a passage, they should be given a new purpose or a new group of questions that influences that reading.

- **Annotation:** During at least one reading of the passage, students should annotate, or make notes on, the text. Annotation focuses students' attention on the text and allows them to track their thought processes as they read. It also allows students to interact with the text by noting words, phrases, or ideas that confuse or interest them. When writing about or discussing a text, students can consult their annotations and retrieve valuable information.

    For more information about annotation, see pages 6–7 of this guide.

- **Additional Tasks:** Collaboration allows students to discuss and problem-solve with their partner peers. An emphasis is placed on demonstrating an understanding of unfamiliar words in context and applying academic vocabulary in new ways. Throughout, students are prompted to cite evidence to support claims and reinforce arguments. Often, students are asked to illustrate written information or connect text to visuals. A section of peer-led activities (pages 88–91) encourages students to ask and answer peer-generated questions.

The TDQs

- ✓ general
- ✓ key details
- ✓ word choice
- ✓ sequence
- ✓ structure
- ✓ purpose
- ✓ inference
- ✓ opinion

Text-dependent questions (TDQs) emphasize what the text has to offer as opposed to the students' personal experiences. This helps students focus on the text — from the literal (what it says) to the structural (how it works) to the inferential (what it means).

The TDQs in this resource ask students to demonstrate a wide range of understanding about the text. There is a progression from questions that ask for general understanding to those that require deeper levels of focus. The first question or two are relatively easy to answer, as this promotes student confidence and lessens the possibility for discouragement or disengagement. Subsequent questions delve into increasingly higher-order involvement in the text. Students are asked why a passage is written the way it is and if they feel that the author's choices were ultimately successful. This type of instruction and questioning not only makes students better readers, it also makes them better writers as they consider the decisions authors make and the effects those choices have on the text and the reader.

All About Annotation
Teacher Instructions

Annotation is the practice of making notes on a text during reading, and it is a crucial component of the close-reading process. It allows students to more deeply dissect a text and make note of the parts that intrigue or excite them, as well as the parts that confuse or disengage them. Annotation gives students a tool with which to interact with the text on their terms and in ways specific to their needs and interests.

Tips and Strategies

- ☑ This resource has been designed to give your students the space needed to annotate the reading passages. Extra space has been included in the margin to the left of the passage. In addition, room has also been added between each line of text, with even more space included between paragraphs.

- ☑ Share the student sample (page 7) to give your students an idea of what is expected of them and how annotation works. This sample only shows three basic ways of annotating: circling unfamiliar words, underlining main ideas, and writing key details. Begin with these to ensure that students understand the concept. Additional responsibilities and tasks can be added later.

- ☑ Much like the skill of summarization requires restraint, so does annotation. Give students a goal. For example, tell them they can only underline one main idea per paragraph and/or their key notes for each paragraph can be no more than five words in length. If these expectations aren't given, students might make too many notes, circle too many words, and underline too much text. This would make the text more difficult to read and create the opposite effect of what is intended.

- ☑ If you see that a majority of your students are circling the same unfamiliar words and noting confusion in the same areas of the text, spend more time and focus on these parts.

- ☑ Instruct students to reference their annotations when answering more complex questions, such as those inquiring about the structural and inferential elements of the text.

- ☑ Annotations can be used as an assessment tool to determine how well students are analyzing a text or even how well they are following directions.

- ☑ If students need more room to annotate, consider allowing them to affix sticky notes onto their pages and add notes in this way.

- ☑ As students become more fluent at the skill of annotating, increase their responsibilities and/or add new tasks. Here are a few examples to consider:
    - ♦ Add a question mark (?) for information they find confusing.
    - ♦ Add an exclamation point (!) for information they find surprising.
    - ♦ Draw arrows between ideas and/or elements to show connections.
    - ♦ Keep track of characters' names and relationships.
    - ♦ Add notes about such elements of authorial craft as tone, mood, or style.

All About Annotation (cont.)
Student Sample

Annotation = making notes on a text as you read it

3 Basic Ways to Annotate a Text

Note key details.
In the left margin, write a few words that give key details from the paragraph. Your notes in this space should be brief. They should be five words or fewer.

Circle difficult words.
If you aren't sure what a word means, circle it. Once you determine its meaning, write the word's definition in the left margin and circle it.

Underline main ideas.
Find the main idea of each paragraph and underline it. The main idea gives the most important information the author is trying to tell you in that paragraph.

Dead-Tree Wishes

1 Once upon a time, a man was in a forest. The man was a woodcutter. <u>The woodcutter came upon a dead tree.</u> The tree was huge and had lots of branches, but it had no (foliage). There was not one speck of green on it. It did not have even the tiniest leaf! The woodcutter raised his ax. Before he could take his first chop, a woodpecker flew down and spoke.

(green leaves)

in forest
man raised ax
woodpecker spoke

2 "Please," the woodpecker said. "Everyone thinks dead trees aren't important. That's not true. Look at all the holes in the trunk and branches. We woodpeckers make our homes in the holes. <u>We need dead trees!</u>"

Dead-Tree Wishes

 Once upon a time, a man was in a forest. The man was a woodcutter. The woodcutter came upon a dead tree. The tree was huge and had lots of branches, but it had no foliage. There was not one speck of green on it. It did not have even the tiniest leaf! The woodcutter raised his ax. Before he could take his first chop, a woodpecker flew down and spoke.

 "Please," the woodpecker said. "Everyone thinks dead trees aren't important. That's not true. Look at all the holes in the trunk and branches. We woodpeckers make our homes in the holes. We need dead trees!"

 The man agreed to spare the tree. The woodpecker said, "You are doing a good deed. For your kind act, I will grant you a couple of wishes."

 The woodcutter was happy. He had always dreamed of having a beach house and a new car. He raced home to tell his children. When they heard about the wishes, they started crying for things they wanted. "We want phones and bikes! We want candy and games! We want to be king and queen of the world!"

 The woodcutter covered his ears. "I wish you would all be quiet!" he cried.

 The children were quiet all right, but something was very wrong. The children's mouths were sealed shut! They could no longer open their lips. The woodcutter looked at his children. He thought, "Poor children! Maybe I should wish for phones and bikes. Maybe I should wish for candy and games. Maybe I should wish that they were king and queen."

 Then he thought, "No, I am not going to give them what they want. The wish is mine. I am going to wish for what I want."

 "For my last wish," the woodcutter said, "I wish my first wish undone."

UNIT **1**

Close-Reading Tasks

Your Name: _____   Partner: _____

Dead-Tree Wishes (cont.)

First — Silently read "Dead Tree Wishes." You might see words you do not know. There might be parts you do not understand. Keep reading! Try to find out what the story is mainly about.

Then — Sum up the story. Write the main actions and most important information. If someone reads your summary, that person should know it is this story you are writing about.

_____
_____
_____
_____
_____

After That — Read the story again. Use a pencil to circle or mark words you don't know. Note places that confuse you. Underline the main action or idea of each paragraph.

Next — Meet with your partner. Help each other find these words in the text.

      spare   deed   grant   sealed

Read the sentences around the words. Think about how they fit in the whole story. Write what the words mean. Which information from the text helped you figure out the meaning of the words? The first row of the chart is done for you.

Word	What It Means	Information That Helps
spare	to not hurt or harm; to leave alone	The woodcutter didn't cut down the tree.
deed		
grant		
sealed		

©Teacher Created Resources

UNIT **1**

Text-Dependent Questions

Your Name: _____

Dead-Tree Wishes (cont.)

Now Answer the story questions below.

1. Why do woodpeckers need dead trees? _____
   _____

2. Why were the children quiet? _____

   Imagine you had to be quiet for the same reason the children were. What might happen to you? What problems would you have?
   _____
   _____

3. Draw two trees. One tree should be dead. The other tree should have some foliage on it.

    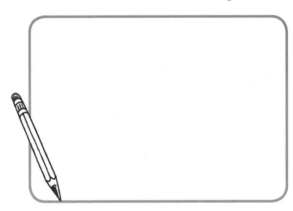

   How do you know the dead tree has no foliage? Rewrite the part of the story that tells you.
   _____
   _____

4. The story tells us the woodcutter has two children. It does not say if they are boys or girls. Use clues from the story to make your best guess. Fill in the circle beside your guess.

   The woodcutter's children are probably . . .

   Ⓐ two boys   Ⓑ two girls   Ⓒ one boy and one girl

   Which clue in the story helped you guess this? Write the clue.
   _____
   _____

#2691 Close Reading with Text-Dependent Questions

UNIT **1**

Your Name: _____

Dead-Tree Wishes (cont.)

Then) Reread the entire story one last time.

5. Write down the first four words in the first paragraph.
   _____

   Why do you think the author began the story this way?
   _____
   _____

6. How does the author make you think the children might not be okay?
   _____
   _____

   Why do you think the author wanted you to think the children might not be okay?
   _____
   _____

7. When do you find out the children are going to be okay? What happens in the story to give you this information?
   _____
   _____

   Do you think it is important that the author lets you know the children will be okay? Why or why not? How would the story be different if you were not given this information?
   _____
   _____
   _____

 Learn More — Use books or the Internet to look up facts about woodpeckers. See if you can find out how many times they tap in a day!

Going, Going, Gone!

1. There were about 800. They swam in the ocean. They ate fish. They came to land when it was time to make a nest. First, they made a burrow. Then, they laid their eggs in the little holes they had tunneled. When the eggs hatched, their chicks were safe and dry in the burrow.

2. Disaster struck! The burrows were no longer safe. The chicks were in danger. The adult birds were in danger, too. In one night alone, about 180 birds were lost! Disaster struck again and again. More and more birds were killed. Soon there were fewer than 10 birds left! Soon they would all be gone.

3. The birds that needed saving are called little penguins. Little penguins are the smallest kind of penguin. They lived on Middle Island. Middle Island is on the Southern coast of Australia. Disaster struck when people brought foxes to the mainland. The foxes were not native to Australia. They were not always there. They were imported to the Australian mainland. The foxes then walked over to Middle Island during low tide. When the tide is low, the water between the mainland and the island is only six inches deep.

4. The foxes had been imported so people could hunt them. The foxes hunted, too! The penguins are small. They cannot fly. It is easy for the foxes to prey on them. Then a farmer had an idea. He had a dog imported from Italy. It was a Maremma sheepdog. This kind of dog can be trained to live with a group of animals. Then it protects these animals. The farmer wanted to train the dog to protect the penguins.

5. The idea worked! The dog kept the penguins safe! Today, two Maremma sheepdogs work at a time. They stay with the penguins during breeding season. They work day and night for five days. Then they get two days off!

UNIT **2**

Close-Reading Tasks

Your Name: _____

Going, Going, Gone! *(cont.)*

First — Silently read "Going, Going, Gone!" You might see words you do not know or parts you do not understand. Keep reading! Try to find out what the story is mainly about.

Then — Sum up the story. Write the main actions and most important information. If someone reads your summary, that person should know it is this story in the book you are writing about, not a different story!

_____

_____

_____

_____

After That — Read the story again. Use a pencil to circle or mark words you don't know. Note places that confuse you. Underline the main action or idea of each paragraph.

Next — Meet with your partner. Help each other find these words in the text.

disaster   native   imported

Read the sentences around the words. Think and talk about what the words mean. Work together to do the following:

- Think of some natural **disasters**.
- Think of some **native** animals.
- Think of some **imported** animals. (**Hint:** You might only see these animals in zoos.)

Then look at the words below. Decide which one could most likely be a disaster, a native animal, and an imported animal. Tell why.

Word	What Is It?	Explain
deer		
earthquake		
tiger		

©*Teacher Created Resources*   13   #2691 *Close Reading with Text-Dependent Questions*

UNIT **2**

Text-Dependent Questions

Your Name: _____

Going, Going, Gone! *(cont.)*

Now Answer the story questions below.

1. How did the foxes get on Middle Island? _____
   _____
   _____

2. Today, there are hundreds of penguins on Middle Island. Tell why.
   _____
   _____
   _____

3. In paragraph 1, you are told that penguins "laid their eggs in the little holes they had tunneled." Use those words to help you draw a penguin's burrow.

   [drawing box]

   Foxes can't climb trees, so why didn't the penguins build their nests in trees? Use information from the story to answer.
   _____
   _____

4. Compare the work week of the sheepdogs to your school week. How are these two weeks alike? How are they different?
   _____
   _____
   _____

UNIT 2

More TDQs

Your Name: _____

Going, Going, Gone! (cont.)

Then — Reread the entire story one last time. Think about the title as you read.

5. What is the second paragraph mainly about?

_____
_____
_____

6. If you only read the title and then through just the second paragraph, how would you feel? Would you be afraid none of the penguins lived?

_____
_____
_____

7. In which paragraph do you know for sure that the penguins are safe from the foxes? Fill in the bubble beside the correct answer.

　　○ 1　　　○ 2　　　○ 3　　　○ 4　　　○ 5

Find one sentence from the paragraph that proves this. Quote that sentence here:

_____
_____

Why do you think the author waited until this point to tell you the penguins were safe? Do you think it made the story better? (There is no wrong answer! It is what you think!)

_____
_____
_____
_____

Learn More — Find pictures of little penguins and Maremma sheepdogs. List at least five differences between them. Write on the back of this paper.

©Teacher Created Resources

Helping Hands

 Darcy (begging): Mom, Mom, take this! I don't want to carry it anymore. My arms are going to break off. It must weigh a ton.

Darcy's Mom (laughing): Darling, I don't think a stuffed lion weighs 2,000 pounds, but I'll take it. Give it to me. I can hold it in my left hand.

 Darcy (gratefully): Thanks, Mom! I really appreciate you helping me. I'm really grateful. You're better than a month of Saturdays!

Darcy's Mom (smiling): Thank you, but keep moving. We can't be late.

 Darcy (pleading): Mom, Mom, I'm begging you to take this, too! It's impossible for me to carry it any farther. I'm afraid I'm going to drop it, and it will shatter like glass. We'll never be able to put it back together.

Darcy's Mom (sternly): I don't think a stuffed octopus can shatter like glass. Here, put it in my right hand. I'm only going to carry it because I need you to walk faster.

 Darcy (appreciatively): Thanks, Mom. You're the best mom ever!

Darcy's Mom (sternly): Actions speak louder than words. Walk faster!

 Darcy (crying): Mom, carry this for me! I can't tote it any farther. It must weigh as much as a ton of bricks!

Darcy's Mom (even more sternly): Stop making a scene. You're the one that wanted to bring all your stuffed animals. Okay, give it to me. I'll carry your stuffed horse, but no more! All of my hands are full.

 Darcy (sobbing): Mom, Mom, I can't go on anymore. I can't go another step. Please, please pick me up and carry me!

Darcy's Mom (angrily): Darcy, how am I supposed to do that? I'm carrying something of yours in my left hand, right hand, and middle hand! You know I only have three hands!

UNIT 3 — Close-Reading Tasks

Your Name: _____ Partner: _____

Helping Hands (cont.)

First — Silently read "Helping Hands." You might see words you do not know. There might be parts you do not understand. Keep reading! Try to find out what the story is mainly about.

Then — Sum up the play. Write the main actions and most important information. If someone reads your summary, that person should know it is this play you are writing about.

_____
_____
_____
_____
_____
_____

After That — Read the play again. Use a pencil to circle or mark words you don't know. Note places that confuse you. Underline the main action or idea of each paragraph.

Next — Meet with your partner. Look at all the words in the parentheses that describe the character's tone of voice when they are speaking. Use what the characters say to help you define the words. Then write a phrase or a sentence you might say if you were speaking with the same tone of voice. The first one is done for you.

Word	Meaning	Sentence
grateful	to be thankful	I am grateful that I had cereal for breakfast instead of fried ants!
plead		
stern		
appreciate		

©Teacher Created Resources

UNIT 3

Text-Dependent Questions

Your Name: _____

Helping Hands (cont.)

Now) Answer the story questions below.

1. What did Darcy's mom carry in each hand? Write three sentences.

    a. Use these words in your first sentence: first   left

    _____

    _____

    b. Use these words in your second sentence: next   right

    _____

    _____

    c. Use these words in your third sentence: then   middle

    _____

    _____

2. Darcy feels her lion weighs a ton. When do you find out how much a ton weighs? Quote what the character says.

    _____

    _____

3. Darcy says her stuffed horse weighs as much as "a ton of bricks." Tell if this is possible or not. Defend your answer by using information from the text.

    _____

    _____

4. Darcy tells her mom that she is better than "a month of Saturdays." Is she saying something nice about her mother? Tell why or why not.

    _____

    _____

    Why do you think Darcy said "a month of Saturdays" instead of "a month of Mondays"?

    _____

    _____

UNIT 3

Your Name: _____

Helping Hands (cont.)

Then — Reread the entire story one last time.

5. What do you find out when Darcy's mom speaks for the last time? On the lines, tell what you find out. In the box, show this information by drawing a picture of it.

   _____
   _____
   _____
   _____

6. How do Darcy's mom's last words show us that the story is not realistic fiction? **Realistic fiction** stories are made up, but they follow the rules of the world we live in.

   _____
   _____

   Do you think Darcy's mom's last words made the story better? Explain why or why not.

   _____
   _____

7. **Foreshadowing** is when an author gives a hint about something that will happen. In section #5 of the story, Darcy's mom says "All of my hands are full." How does this foreshadow (give a hint about) what we learn about her in section #6 of the story?

   _____
   _____

   If Darcy's mom only had two hands, what would she probably have said instead of "All of my hands are full"?

   _____

 Learn More — Darcy's mom says, "Actions speak louder than words." This phrase is an idiom. With your teacher, look up the meaning of the word *idiom* and examples of other idioms. On the back of your paper, write about the idiom "Actions speak louder than words." You can explain what it means, or you can create an example that shows what it means.

Biscuit Drop

 Bob Bates dropped some biscuits. He didn't drop them by accident. He dropped them on purpose. They didn't just drop off the table or from his hand. Bates dropped them from a second-floor window! It was raining outside. Bates left the biscuits that had dropped to the ground. He left them outside in the rain overnight.

 Bates was testing the biscuits for two things. First, he wanted to see how easily they would crack. He wanted biscuits that were hardy and didn't crack easily. Next, he wanted biscuits that were resistant to water. He didn't want biscuits that got soggy too easily.

 Bates was part of an expedition. He was part of a team going to K2. K2 is the second highest mountain in the world. The summit of K2 is 28,251 feet high. The Death Zone starts at about 26,247 feet. That means the top of the K2 is in the Death Zone. The Death Zone is a place where there is not enough oxygen for humans to breathe.

 The year was 1937. No one had climbed K2 yet. The ascent was too hard. Mt. Everest is the highest mountain, but it is easier to climb. It is not as steep. It is not as hard to get to the top. There is a well-worn route to the summit of Mt. Everest. There is no easy route to the top of K2.

 One of Bates' jobs was to look after all the food for the expedition. He had to select it. Then he had to buy it. Bates ordered 100 pounds of the same brand of biscuits. Bates knew it was the right brand because of his tests. Bates went on two expeditions to K2. He did not reach the top. No one reached the top until 1954.

UNIT 4

Close-Reading Tasks

Your Name: _____ Partner: _____

Biscuit Drop (cont.)

First — Silently read "Biscuit Drop." You might see words you do not know. There might be parts you do not understand. Keep reading! Try to find out what the story is mainly about.

Then — Sum up the story. Write the main actions and most important information. If someone reads your summary, that person should know it is this story you are writing about.

_____
_____
_____
_____
_____
_____

After That — Read the story again. Use a pencil to circle or mark words you don't know. Note places that confuse you. Underline the main action or idea of each paragraph.

Next — Meet with your partner. Help each other find these words in the text.

hardy   resistant   expedition   route

Read the sentences around the words. Think about how they fit in the whole story. Write what the words mean. Which information from the text helped you and your partner figure out the meaning of the words? The first row of the chart is done for you.

Word	What Is It?	Explain
hardy	tough, strong, doesn't crack or break easily	Bates wanted hardy biscuits, so he tested them by dropping them out of a window.
resistant		
expedition		
route		

©Teacher Created Resources   21   #2691 Close Reading with Text-Dependent Questions

UNIT 4

Text-Dependent Questions

Your Name: _____

Biscuit Drop (cont.)

Now — Answer the story questions below.

1. How did Bates test his biscuits? _____
   _____

2. Most likely, what were the biscuits on the expedition to K2 like?
   _____

   What facts from the story helped you answer the question above?
   _____
   _____
   _____

3. Why is the highest mountain in the world easier to climb than K2? Give two reasons. Quote words from the story for each reason.

   Reason #1: _____

   Reason #2: _____

4. Look at the picture of the mountain. Circle the part of the mountain that is its summit. On the lines to the right, explain how the story helped you know which part to circle.

   _____
   _____
   _____
   _____
   _____

   Once climbers get near the summit of K2, they might have a difficult time there. Why? Use evidence from the story to support your answer.

   _____
   _____

UNIT 4

More TDQs

Your Name: _____

Biscuit Drop (cont.)

Then — Reread the entire story one last time. Pay attention to how some paragraphs do not talk about the biscuits.

5. Biscuits are mentioned in which three paragraphs? Fill in the bubbles beside the correct paragraph numbers.

   ○ 1   ○ 2   ○ 3   ○ 4   ○ 5

   What are the other two paragraphs mainly about?

   _____
   _____

6. In which paragraph do we learn *why* Bates threw biscuits out a second-floor window?

   ○ 1   ○ 2   ○ 3   ○ 4   ○ 5

   Why do you think the author told you when she did?

   _____
   _____
   _____

7. Bates did not make it to the top of K2. Do you think his choice of biscuits was the reason? Why or why not? Use clues from the story to answer this question.

   _____
   _____
   _____
   _____

Learn More — Look in books or use the Internet to find out more information about K2 and some of the people who have climbed it or tried to climb it. What do climbers use in the Death Zone to help them breathe?

_____
_____

©Teacher Created Resources

#2691 Close Reading with Text-Dependent Questions

Animal Facts

 Rabbit boasted, "I know everything! Ask me questions about animals. I'll answer all of them!" Tortoise was tired of Rabbit always showing off, so she decided to ask some hard questions. Tortoise didn't think Rabbit would know the answers.

 Tortoise said, "Okay, I will. First, what color socks does Bear wear? Second, which animal can jump higher than a house? Third, which side of Cheetah has the most spots? Finally, how many books can Owl put in his empty backpack?" Tortoise was going to ask some more questions, but Rabbit interrupted.

 "Even a baby could answer those questions," Rabbit sneered. "They aren't hard questions at all. They're all as easy as pie. Bear's socks aren't any color, because bears don't wear socks. They have bare feet! Second, all animals can jump higher than a house. Houses can't jump! The answer to the third question is not the left side. It is not the right side. It is the outside! Owl can only put one book in his empty backpack. After that, the backpack isn't empty."

 Tortoise didn't sneer at Rabbit. She did the opposite. She complimented her. "You're clever, Rabbit!" she said. "You knew *bear* and *bare* are homonyms. *Bear* and *bare* are words that sound the same. They sound the same, but they have different meanings. I did not think you knew that."

 "I'll bet you don't know this," jeered Rabbit. "I can make something. I can make it bigger and bigger. No matter how big I make it, it always weighs the same. I bet you don't know what it is I can make." Rabbit had to stop jeering when Tortoise answered. There was no reason to sneer or make fun of Tortoise because Tortoise knew. The answer was "a hole." Rabbit could make a hole bigger and bigger. The hole would always weigh the same. It would always weigh nothing.

UNIT **5**

Close-Reading Tasks

Your Name: _____   Partner: _____

Animal Facts (cont.)

First — Silently read "Animal Facts." You might see words you do not know. There might be parts you do not understand. Keep reading! Try to find out what the story is mainly about.

Then — Sum up the story. Write the main actions and most important information. If someone reads your summary, that person should know it is this story you are writing about.

_____
_____
_____
_____
_____
_____

After That — Read the story again. Use a pencil to circle or mark words you don't know. Note places that confuse you. Underline the main action or idea of each paragraph.

Next — Meet with your partner. Help each other find these words in the text.

boasted   sneered   jeered   homonym

Read the sentences around the words. Think about how they fit in the whole story. Write what the words mean. Which information in the text helps you and your partner figure out the meaning of the words? The first row of the chart is done for you.

Word	What It Means	Information That Helps
boasted	to show off about what you know, own, or can do	Rabbit boasted that she knew everything.
sneered		
jeered		
homonym		

©Teacher Created Resources   25   #2691 Close Reading with Text-Dependent Questions

UNIT 5 — Text-Dependent Questions

Your Name: _____

Animal Facts (cont.)

Now Answer the story questions below.

1. Who is more well-mannered, Rabbit or Tortoise? Tell why. Use some of your vocabulary words in your answer.

   _____

   _____

2. Which riddle does Tortoise ask first? _____

   _____

   Explain what you have to know for the answer to make sense.

   _____

   _____

3. In paragraph 3, Rabbit says the riddles are "as easy as pie." What does Rabbit mean?

   _____

   Quote one sentence from the text that shows your answer above is correct.

   _____

   _____

4. Imagine if Tortoise asked Rabbit, "What did one bee say to another bee?" Imagine that Rabbit answered, "Just be (bee) yourself!" Most likely, what would Tortoise do? Would she sneer at Rabbit, or would she compliment her? Check the box beside your answer.

   ❏ sneer   ❏ compliment

   Now use evidence from the story to support your answer. _____

   _____

   Write down something you think Tortoise might say when Rabbit got the right answer.

   _____

   _____

#2691 Close Reading with Text-Dependent Questions

UNIT **5**

More TDQs

Your Name: _____

Animal Facts (cont.)

Then Reread the entire story one last time. Think about the title as you read.

5. Does the title make it seem as if the story is going to be fiction or nonfiction? Why?

   _____
   _____

   When and how do you first begin to get a hint that the story does not fit with the title in this way?

   _____
   _____
   _____

6. Write a new and better title for the story.

   _____

   Tell why your title fits the story better.

   _____
   _____

7. Which of these two riddles has a homonym in its answer? Fill in the circle beside your answer. Then explain your answer.

   Ⓐ Why did Rabbit sit on her watch? **She wanted to be on time.**

   Ⓑ What part of the month sounds like it has no strength? **the week**

   _____
   _____
   _____

Learn More Work with a partner. Do one of the following:

☐ Work together to make a list of homonyms. Can you think of at least 10?

☐ Write five sentences about rabbits or tortoises. Four of your sentences should be real facts. One should be fiction. Can your classmates spot the one that is fiction?

©Teacher Created Resources 27 #2691 Close Reading with Text-Dependent Questions

Edward Lear

1 Picture this: a man with a beard.

Now picture this: a man with a beard with bird nests in it!

2 Most likely, your first picture was somewhat normal. You might have pictured someone you know or someone you've seen before. What about your second image? Most likely you did not picture something you have seen before! You can't have seen bird nests in a beard before! It is ridiculous to think that birds would make a nest in a beard! It is too silly to be true.

3 Edward Lear was a poet. In 1836 he published a book of poems. The book was called *A Book of Nonsense*. It was filled with silly poems, like this one:

> There was an Old Man with a beard,
>
> Who said, "It is just as I feared! —
>
> Two Owls and a Hen,
>
> Four Larks and a Wren,
>
> Have all built their nests in my beard.

4 Lear's silly poems made people laugh. They made people happy. Maybe Lear wanted to write happy things because some things in his life were not happy. Lear's parents had 21 children! They were too poor to take care of all of them. When Lear was only four years old, he was sent to live with his oldest sister, Ann. She was 21 years older than him.

5 Lear also had frequent seizures. He would fall to the ground and suffer a fit of shaking. Lear's seizures started when he was only six years old. When Lear was little, people didn't know what caused the seizures or how to stop them. Today, we know a lot more about them. We know there is nothing shameful about having seizures. We know the seizures are caused by our brains. We know it is no one's fault. Sadly, Lear was ashamed of his many seizures. He blamed himself. He didn't know that it was not his fault.

UNIT **6** Close-Reading Tasks

Your Name: _____   Partner: _____

Edward Lear (cont.)

First — Silently read "Edward Lear." You might see words you do not know. There might be parts you do not understand. Keep reading! Try to find out what the story is mainly about.

Then — Sum up the story. Write the main actions and most important information. If someone reads your summary, that person should know it is this story you are writing about.

_____

_____

_____

_____

_____

_____

After That — Read the story again. Use a pencil to circle or mark words you don't know. Note places that confuse you. Underline the main action or idea of each paragraph.

Next — Meet with your partner. Help each other find these words in the text.

        ridiculous   frequent

Read the sentences around the words. Think about how they fit in the whole story. Think about what the words could mean. Then use what you know to fill in the blanks together.

    a. If something is **ridiculous**, it is _____.

    b. Why would it be ridiculous to wear ice skates to school? _____

_____

_____

    c. If something is **frequent**, it happens _____.

    d. How frequently does your class go to the library? _____

_____

_____

©Teacher Created Resources

UNIT **6**

Text-Dependent Questions

Your Name: _____

Edward Lear *(cont.)*

Now Answer the story questions below.

1. Even if the poem about the man and his beard were not in a book titled *The Book of Nonsense*, you would have known that it was nonsense. What clues does it give you that tell you this?

   _____
   _____
   _____

2. Quote the part of the poem that tells you what kind of birds made the nests.

   _____
   _____

   How many birds were there in total? Write the number on the line. Draw that number of birds in the box.

   _____

3. How does the story say Lear felt when he had a seizure?

   _____

   Do you think Lear should have felt this way? Tell why.

   _____
   _____

4. Do you think Lear had a good imagination? What parts of the story helped you form your opinion of Lear's imagination?

   _____
   _____
   _____

UNIT **6**

More TDQs

Your Name: _____

Edward Lear (cont.)

Then — Reread the entire story one last time. Pay attention to how the last two paragraphs differ from the rest of the passage.

5. A biography tells about someone's life. A biography is written by someone about someone else. Which paragraphs in the story are biographical? Fill in the bubble beside your answers.

    ○ 1   ○ 2   ○ 3   ○ 4   ○ 5

    Name two important things you are told about Lear's life in this part of the story.

    a. _____

    _____

    b. _____

    _____

6. Limericks are special types of poems. They have five lines. The lines rhyme a special way. The 1st, 2nd, and 5th lines rhyme. The 3rd and 4th lines rhyme.

    First, go back to the poem. Underline the last word in each line.

    Next, tell how you know this poem is a limerick. In your answer, include line count and what exact words from the poem rhyme.

    _____

    _____

    _____

7. The first thing the author asked you to do was picture two things in your head. Do you think that was a good way to start the story? Did it help you get ready for the poem? Explain.

    _____

    _____

    _____

Learn More — Edward Lear is famous for his nonsense story "The Owl and the Pussy-Cat." Find a copy. Listen to it or read it. On another piece of paper, draw a picture of one part of this story.

©Teacher Created Resources   31   #2691 Close Reading with Text-Dependent Questions

Horribly Sick

 Mrs. Danza looked at her son Carlos. She was concerned. "Oh no," she sighed, "He's doing it again. I just don't understand it. I've never seen any child act like this before. It's not normal. I'm so worried. He must be horribly sick. I'll take him to the doctor."

 Mrs. Danza walked up to her son. "Carlos," she said firmly, "I need you to put that down." Carlos kept his head down. He didn't respond. He didn't even react when Mrs. Danza said his name very loudly. Mrs. Danza took what Carlos was holding in his hands. Only then did Carlos look up.

 "Did you know, Mom," Carlos said, "that kangaroos are marsupials?" Mrs. Danza looked fearfully at Carlos. As she listened to him chatter on, she was afraid he had lost his mind. "Yes," he said, "marsupials are mammals like us, but they are special kinds of mammals that carry their babies in pouches. Kangaroos are the largest marsupials in the world. Baby kangaroos are called joeys. At times, kangaroos can jump three times their own height! They can hop around quickly on two feet or walk slowly on four feet. They can't walk backwards. Oh, and they can swim."

 When Mrs. Danza took Carlos to the doctor, the doctor looked at Carlos. Mrs. Danza described Carlos's symptoms. "I know he's sick," she said. "He just sits all day doing the same thing. It makes him lose his mind. It makes him talk nonsense. Just this morning, he told me a group of kangaroos is called a mob or a troop!"

 The doctor looked at what Carlos was doing. He told Mrs. Danza that Carlos's symptoms were not a sign of any illness or disease. He said what Carlos was doing was just fine. "But I don't understand," Mrs. Danza said. "How can that be normal? All the other children play video games or watch TV. He just reads books. How can he ever learn anything?"

UNIT **7**

Close-Reading Tasks

Your Name: _____ Partner: _____

Horribly Sick (cont.)

First — Silently read "Horribly Sick." You might see words you do not know. There might be parts you do not understand. Keep reading! Try to find out what the story is mainly about.

Then — Sum up the story. Write the main actions and most important information. If someone reads your summary, that person should know it is this story you are writing about.

_____
_____
_____
_____
_____

After That — Read the story again. Use a pencil to circle or mark words you don't know. Note places that confuse you. Underline the main action or idea of each paragraph.

Next — Meet with your partner. Help each other find these words in the text.

    concerned   respond   react   chatter   symptoms

Read the sentences around the words. Think about how they fit in the whole story. Think about what the words mean. Then circle the correct **bolded** word(s) below. Next, tell how the story helped you know the answer. The first one is done for you.

a. If you're <u>concerned</u>, you are (**worried**)　**not worried**　about something.
We know this because _____Mrs. Danza is worried about Carlos._____

b. If you <u>respond</u>, you　**react**　**don't react**　in some way. We know this because
_____

c. If you <u>chatter</u>, you　**talk**　**don't talk** . We know this because _____
_____

d. <u>Symptoms</u> are　**signs**　**not signs**　of something. We know this because
_____

©Teacher Created Resources

UNIT 7

Text-Dependent Questions

Your Name: _____

Horribly Sick (cont.)

Now Answer the story questions below.

1. What does Mrs. Danza think is normal behavior for children? _____
   _____

   Why did she think this is normal? _____
   _____

2. Mrs. Danza asked how Carlos could learn anything from reading books. Prove Mrs. Danza wrong by writing down at least three things Carlos learned about kangaroos.
   _____
   _____
   _____

3. Use *only* information given in the story to answer these three questions:

   a. To which group do both humans and kangaroos belong? Check the correct box.

      ❑ marsupials   ❑ mammals   ❑ reptiles

   b. How are human mothers different from kangaroo mothers?
      _____
      _____

   c. How are you different from a young kangaroo?
      _____
      _____

4. What does Carlos do when Mrs. Danza says his name very loudly?
   _____

   Why might he have reacted this way? _____
   _____

UNIT **7** — More TDQs

Your Name: _____

Horribly Sick *(cont.)*

Then — Reread the entire story one last time.

5. What do you find out about Carlos and his mother in the last paragraph?

_____

_____

6. For the story to have the same surprise ending, did Carlos have to be reading a book about kangaroos? Why or why not?

_____

_____

Imagine you are the author. Think of a different topic Carlos could have been reading about. Pick a topic that you think would have made the story more interesting. Write two pieces of information on that topic that you could tell Mrs. Danza.

Topic: _____

Information: First, _____

Second, _____

7. Reread the third paragraph. Underline this sentence: "Mrs. Danza took what Carlos was holding in his hands." Now rewrite this sentence so that there is no surprise ending.

_____

Would you have liked the story better if the author used this rewritten line in the third paragraph? Why or why not?

_____

_____

Learn More — You are told a group of kangaroos is a mob or a troop. Can you find out what groups of these animals are called? Create a chart like this one.

whales _____	chickens _____	zebras _____	lions _____
mosquitos _____	geese _____	bats _____	ants _____

Crocodile Tears

 Snap! The crocodile's jaws snapped shut! Having caught its lunch, the crocodile began to consume it. As the reptile ate its lunch, it began to cry. Tears ran out of its eyes. Why was the crocodile crying? Was it sad that it was consuming a meal? Did it feel sorry for its prey?

 Crocodiles do not cry when they are sad. They do not cry when they are happy. They do not have emotions the way people do. Crocodiles cry because it is good for them. The tears help them in many ways. For one thing, the tears clean their eyes. The tears also help get rid of extra salt the crocodiles take in with their food. In addition to these two things, the tears also help keep a crocodile's eyes from drying out.

 People can be said to cry crocodile tears. "Crying crocodile tears" is an expression. We use it when someone is not expressing real emotion. We use these words when we talk about someone who is crying fake tears. Someone may pretend to be sad or upset. The expression came about because crocodiles will often shed tears as they eat. The crocodiles may look sad, but they are not sad. It is just that the act of eating starts the tears flowing.

 There is still one more case in which all is not what it seems when it comes to crocodiles. Crocodiles have the strongest bite of any animal. Think of a great white shark. A crocodile can clamp down with even more force than a fully grown great white shark! If this is true, how is it possible that people can hold crocodile's mouths shut with their bare hands? Are we being tricked when we see this?

 Think about what you see. A person could not hold a crocodile's mouth open! They can hold it shut! A crocodile has strong jaw muscles for clamping down, but its muscles for opening its jaws are small and weak. These muscles are so weak that a person could indeed hold a crocodile's mouth shut.

UNIT **8**

Close-Reading Tasks

Your Name: _____   Partner: _____

Crocodile Tears (cont.)

First — Silently read "Crocodile Tears." You might see words you do not know. There might be parts you do not understand. Keep reading! Try to find out what the story is mainly about.

Then — Sum up the story. Write the main actions and most important information. If someone reads your summary, that person should know it is this story you are writing about.

_____
_____
_____
_____

After That — Read the story again. Use a pencil to circle or mark words you don't know. Note places that confuse you. Underline the main action or idea of each paragraph.

Next — Meet with your partner. Help each other find these words in the text.

consume   reptile   emotion

Read the sentences around the words. Think about how they fit in the whole story. Discuss what the words mean. Then answer the questions for each word.

a. My partner and I know the meaning of *consume* because in the story

_____

For lunch, we will consume _____

b. My partner and I know that a crocodile is not a mammal because in the story

_____

We can think of two kinds of reptiles: _____ and _____.

c. My partner and I know an emotion is a feeling or state of mind because in the story

_____

We can draw mouths that match the emotion.

happy ○   sad ○

©Teacher Created Resources   37   #2691 Close Reading with Text-Dependent Questions

UNIT **8**

Text-Dependent Questions

Your Name: _____

Crocodile Tears (cont.)

Now Answer the story questions below.

1. Why are some people able to hold a crocodile's mouth shut?

   _____

   _____

2. How are tears good for crocodiles? List three reasons given in the story.

   Reason #1: _____

   Reason #2: _____

   Reason #3: _____

3. If someone says, "Casey is crying crocodile tears," what does that person think Casey is doing?

   _____

   Do you think the person crying crocodile tears is sad? Write down one sentence from the story that helped you answer.

   _____

   _____

4. Whose bite is stronger? For each one, circle the animal that has the stronger bite.

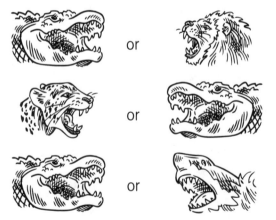

   Find a line from the story that you could use to defend your answers. Write that line here.

   _____

UNIT **8**

Your Name: _____

Crocodile Tears *(cont.)*

Then — Reread the entire story one last time. Pay attention to how paragraph 3 is different from the rest of the passage.

5. In your opinion, which paragraph is the *most* important paragraph in the passage? Fill in the bubble beside your answer and then tell why.

    ○ 1   ○ 2   ○ 3   ○ 4   ○ 5

    _____
    _____

    In your opinion, which paragraph is the *least* important paragraph in the passage? Fill in the bubble beside your answer and then tell why.

    ○ 1   ○ 2   ○ 3   ○ 4   ○ 5

    _____
    _____

6. Is this passage fiction or nonfiction? How do you know? _____
    _____

    Reread the first line of paragraph 3. Imagine this is the *only* line you read in the entire passage. Why might this one line make you think that the passage is fiction?

    _____
    _____

7. You are told in paragraph 1 that crocodiles cry when they eat. You are not told until later *why* crocodiles cry when they eat. Why do you think the writer did this?

    _____
    _____

Learn More — Look in books or on the Internet to find out three more facts about crocodiles. Write your facts on the back of this paper.

Magic Trick

1. Brandon had a whole bag of cookies. He planned to eat the entire bag of cookies by himself. He wasn't going to share. Brandon's big brother Ravi wanted some of the cookies. Brandon told Ravi, "No." He said he wouldn't share. He was very hungry. He was going to eat the entire bag by himself.

2. Ravi told Brandon not to eat the cookies just yet. Ravi told Brandon he would perform a magic trick first. He needed the cookies for the trick. Brandon was mystified. What trick could Ravi perform? How could Ravi do a magic trick with cookies?

3. Ravi got out a plate. Then he told Brandon to put the whole bag of cookies on the plate. Ravi told Brandon to count the cookies. "One, two, three," Brandon began to count. He counted up to 19. "One less than 20," Brandon said. "That is how many cookies there are."

4. Ravi put a hat over the plate of cookies. He said he was going to make all of the cookies disappear without touching the hat. Brandon puzzled over how Ravi could do such a thing. Ravi then waved his hands over the hat. "Ta-da!" he cried. Then he told Brandon that the cookies had disappeared. Brandon was disappointed. He had wanted Ravi to do a real magic trick. He knew the cookies were still there. When Ravi insisted that they were all gone, Brandon got angry. Brandon said he was going to prove  he was right. He reached out and pulled the hat off the plate so Ravi could see all the cookies. Not one was missing.

5. As soon as the hat was off the plate, Ravi smiled. He grabbed the cookies and started eating them. He ate and ate and ate. Soon all the cookies were gone. "The cookies have vanished," he crowed. "I made them all disappear, and I did not touch the hat!"

UNIT 9 — Close-Reading Tasks

Your Name: _____ Partner: _____

Magic Trick (cont.)

First — Silently read "Magic Trick." You might see words you do not know. There might be parts you do not understand. Keep reading! Try to find out what the story is mainly about.

Then — Sum up the story. Write the main actions and most important information. If someone reads your summary, that person should know it is this story you are writing about.

_____
_____
_____
_____
_____

After That — Read the story again. Use a pencil to circle or mark words you don't know. Note places that confuse you. Underline the main action or idea of each paragraph.

Next — Meet with your partner. Help each other find these words in the text.

    entire   mystified   perform   vanished

Pick one word each.

  a. My partner chose the word _____.

    We think that in this passage this word must mean _____
    _____

    We think this because _____
    _____

  b. I chose the word _____.

    We think that in this passage this word must mean _____
    _____

    We think this because _____
    _____

UNIT **9**

Your Name: _____

Magic Trick (cont.)

Now Answer the story questions below.

1. For the trick to work, what had to happen before Ravi could make the cookies disappear?

   _____
   _____

2. In all, how many cookies did Ravi eat?

   a. This number is stated in two different ways in the passage. Write both ways here.

   _____

   b. Write another number phrase for the number of cookies. Your number phrase can use adding or subtracting. Look at the example, but come up with a different one.

   > **Example:** "8 + 11" or "eight plus eleven"

   _____

3. Reread the last paragraph. Find and underline the part where it says that Ravi crowed.

   a. What does Ravi's voice sound like when he crows? Does he sound like a bird or does he sound like he is boasting and showing off?

   _____
   _____

   b. Which parts of the story helped you know this answer?

   _____
   _____

4. Did Ravi really do a magic trick? Explain your answer using evidence from the story.

   _____
   _____
   _____
   _____

UNIT 9 — More TDQs

Your Name: _____

Magic Trick (cont.)

Then Reread the entire story one last time. Pay attention to how the "magic trick" was done.

5. Write a "How To" guide for doing Ravi's magic trick. Show the steps Ravi took to do his trick. Number all your steps. You can have as many steps as you want. The first is written for you.

   Step _1_: Get a plate, some cookies, and a hat.

   Step ___: _____

   Step ___: _____

   Step ___: _____

   Step ___: _____

   Step ___: _____

6. If you read just the first paragraph, who do you think would eat all the cookies? Explain why.

   _____
   _____

7. Rewrite the rest of the last paragraph so that the cookies are shared. The first lines are written for you. Complete the paragraph.

   As soon as the hat was off the plate, Ravi smiled. He started eating cookies.
   _____
   _____
   _____

   Do you like your ending better? Why or why not?

   _____
   _____

Learn More Many magicians wear top hats. Use the Internet or other source to find a picture of a top hat and then draw one on the back of this paper. When you make your drawing, put in a false bottom. Put something under the false bottom!

Alive and Dead

 It can grow everywhere on our bodies except a few places. It can't grow on our lips. It can't grow on the palms of our hands. It can't grow on the soles of our feet. You can see it on other places of your body, but the part you see is not alive. Do you know what it is yet?

 It is your hair. Hair fibers or strands grow from an organ. The organ is in the area under the skin. The organ is called a follicle. The only "living" part of a hair is found in the follicle. Only the part that is growing has living cells. It doesn't hurt to cut your hair, as the part you're cutting has no living cells in it. Can you imagine what it would be like if the hair we saw was made up of living cells?

 Why does hair turn gray? Is it because of stress? Does being worried and upset turn our hair gray? It does not. Each hair has a root and a shaft. The root is in the follicle. We can't see it. The long part or strand we see is called the shaft. The root is surrounded by special cells. The cells make melanin. Melanin is a pigment. It is the pigment that gives hair its color.

 As we age, the cells that make melanin begin to die. Less pigment means the hair becomes more transparent. This means more light can pass through it. It becomes more see-through or clear. Our hair begins to look gray, silver, or white.

 How many scalp follicles do we have? The number varies. It is not the same for everyone. People with blonde hair have the most. They have an average of 150,000 hairs on their head. People with red hair have the least. They have about 90,000. Black- or brown-haired people have 100,000 to 110,000.

UNIT 10

Close-Reading Tasks

Your Name: _____   Partner: _____

Alive and Dead (cont.)

First — Silently read "Alive and Dead." You might see words you do not know. There might be parts you do not understand. Keep reading! Try to find out what the story is mainly about.

Then — Sum up the story. Write the main actions and most important information. If someone reads your summary, that person should know it is this story you are writing about.

_____

_____

_____

_____

After That — Read the story again. Use a pencil to circle or mark words you don't know. Note places that confuse you. Underline the main action or idea of each paragraph.

Next — Meet with your partner. Help each other find these words in the text. Read the sentences around the words. Think about how they fit in the whole story.

follicle   *shaft*   *stress*   *scalp*

Three of these words can be used to label the picture below. Write the correct words on the lines in the picture. Use the information in the story to help you.

Did you feel a lot of **stress** when you wrote the words on the lines? Why or why not?

_____

©Teacher Created Resources   45   #2691 Close Reading with Text-Dependent Questions

UNIT **10**

Text-Dependent Questions

Your Name: _____

Alive and Dead (cont.)

Now Answer the story questions below.

1. Write down three parts of your body where hair **can** grow.

   _____

   _____

   How do you know you are correct? You must use information from the story in your answer.

   _____

   _____

2. Why doesn't it hurt when the hair shaft is cut?

   _____

   _____

3. Imagine a woman who had black hair when she was young. As she aged, this person's hair turned white. Using information from the story, tell why.

   _____

   _____

4. Most likely, if a person had 90,000 hair follicles on his/her scalp, the person's hair would be what color?

   - Draw this person in the box. Color his/her hair the correct color.
   - On the lines, defend your answer by using information from the story.

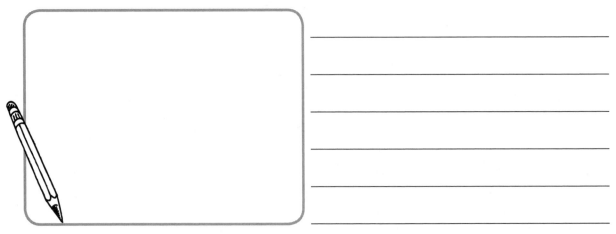

#2691 Close Reading with Text-Dependent Questions

UNIT **10**

Your Name: _____

Alive and Dead (cont.)

Then Reread the entire story one last time. Think about the questions the author asks the reader.

5. How do the questions in paragraphs 1 and 2 differ from the questions in paragraphs 3 and 5? (**Hint:** Think about where the questions can be found in these paragraphs.)

   _____
   _____
   _____

   Why do you think the author asked a question in paragraph 1?

   _____
   _____

6. Do you think the questions in paragraphs 3 and 5 helped you know what the paragraph was going to be mainly about? Tell why or why not.

   _____
   _____
   _____

7. Reread the question asked in paragraph 2. Now use your imagination and answer it! If you want, you can draw a small picture that shows the answer.

   _____
   _____
   _____

Learn More Sea otters have the densest fur of any animal. They can have more hair in one square inch of skin than some people have on their entire heads! Find out more sea otter facts. How does a sea otter's hair help it survive?

A Bare Escape

Andrea was going to be first! Or would it be Danielle? Everyone was sure that Andrea or Danielle would win the race. After all, they were the fastest runners in the school. It was always one or the other who came in first. No one had ever beaten both of them in the same race.

The race course was a big loop. It began and ended at the school, but most of the race was on a trail that went through a small wooded park. When the first runner was spotted coming out of the woods, there was stunned silence. The coach's jaw dropped. No one could believe it. Everyone was too surprised to say a word. Andrea was not in front. Danielle was not the first to run the circle. Ann was in front! Ann had never won a race. Ann usually came in last. No one expected Ann to win. "She must have cheated," someone said quietly.

When Ann stopped at the finish line, she bent over, panting. Her face was pale. Streaks of sweat ran down her face. "I saw a bear!" she said, gasping for breath. "It was big and brown. It dropped on all fours and began to move toward me. I barely escaped!" Once again, there was stunned silence. No one believed Ann. Once again, people wondered if Ann had cheated.

Andrea and Danielle, only a hair's width apart, came into view. Crossing the finish line, they looked at Ann with suspicion. They thought Ann cheated by cutting through the woods. As she had raced passed them, she had told them to run for their lives. She had told them there was a bear, but who could believe that?

Suddenly, a police car drove up. Its lights were flashing. "Everyone inside!" a police officer said loudly. "A bear has escaped from the city zoo. It may be close by. We believe it is in the park or the near vicinity."

UNIT 11

Close-Reading Tasks

Your Name: _____ Partner: _____

A Bare Escape (cont.)

First — Silently read "A Bare Escape." You might see words you do not know. There might be parts you do not understand. Keep reading! Try to find out what the story is mainly about.

Then — Sum up the story. Write the main actions and most important information. If someone reads your summary, that person should know it is this story you are writing about.

_____
_____
_____
_____
_____
_____

After That — Read the story again. Use a pencil to circle or mark words you don't know. Note places that confuse you. Underline the main action or idea of each paragraph.

Next — Meet with your partner. Help each other find these words in the text.

      course   loop   stunned   vicinity

Read the sentences around the words. Think about how they fit in the whole story. Write what the words mean. Which information in the text helps you and your partner figure out the meaning of the words? The first row of the chart is done for you.

Word	What It Means	Information That Helps
course	path, way, or track	The race course was where one ran.
loop		
stunned		
vicinity		

©Teacher Created Resources   49   #2691 Close Reading with Text-Dependent Questions

UNIT **11**

Text-Dependent Questions

Your Name: _____

A Bare Escape (cont.)

Now Answer the story questions below.

1. What did people think at first when they saw that Ann was in front? _____
   _____

   Why did they think this? _____
   _____

2. What was the first thing Ann did once she stopped at the finish line?
   _____

   How do you know Ann ran fast? Quote words or phrases from the story that help you to know.
   _____
   _____

3. It says in the story that when Andrea and Danielle came into view, they were only "a hair's width apart." Does this mean they were very close or very far apart? Explain how you know.
   _____
   _____

4. Think about what the race course looked like. Reread the words about the race course to make sure the picture in your head is correct. In the box, draw a simple map that shows the course. On your map, do the following:

   • Mark the <u>trail</u> with **a solid line**.

   • Label the <u>school</u> and the <u>park</u>.

   • Draw **a dotted line** to show the path Andrea and Danielle thought Ann might have taken.

#2691 Close Reading with Text-Dependent Questions

UNIT **11**

More TDQs

Your Name: _____

A Bare Escape (cont.)

Then Reread the story one last time. Think about how the last paragraph relates to the story.

5. In one or two sentences, tell what you find out in the last paragraph. Use the word *vicinity* in your answer.

_____

_____

_____

6. If you did not read the last paragraph, why might you think Ann cheated?

_____

_____

Did the first paragraph make it easier or harder to think Ann might be cheating? Explain.

_____

_____

_____

7. Sometimes when we are scared, our bodies make *adrenaline*. Adrenaline makes our blood flow faster. It makes us breathe faster. It gets our muscles ready for extra movement. Use this information to discuss Ann passing Andrea and Danielle.

_____

_____

Do you think you had to know about adrenaline to enjoy the story? Tell why or why not.

_____

_____

Learn More Using books or the Internet, find out how fast a bear can run. Can one kind of bear run faster than another? On the back of this paper, write down the information. Then write a sentence telling if you can run faster than a bear!

_____

_____

The Ins and Outs of Doors

1. Learning how to read is a waste of time. That was once my firm opinion. My mother told me I would feel differently one day, but I didn't believe her. I was certain that my opinion would never change.

2. Then two things happened that caused me to alter my opinion. The first thing started with a BAM! A store had two glass doors. The doors were adjacent. One door had the word ENTER on it. The door right next to it had the word EXIT. When I was going into the store, I tried to go in through the door that said EXIT. That's when I hit the glass. It hurt!

3. I had learned a lesson. The door to use always says ENTER. When it was time to leave the store, I was careful. I did not go out the door that said EXIT. I went out the door that was adjacent to it. I went out the door right next to it that said ENTER. At least I *tried* to go out the door that said ENTER. You can imagine what happened to me. Yes, it hurt!

4. Then something worse happened. After hitting the door, I was afraid to go out any of those glass doors. I wasn't going to risk getting hurt a third time, so I went looking for an alternate door. I found another door at the back of the store. This door was a solid, single door. No other door was close to it. I pushed on the handle and started to walk outside.

5. DING! DING! DING! An alarm started to go off! You can imagine how crazy everything got. One firefighter said to me, "Can't you read? It says EMERGENCY EXIT ONLY! ALARM WILL SOUND!" My opinion changed right then and there. I no longer think that learning how to read is a waste of time. On the contrary, I think learning how to read is very important.

UNIT 12

Close-Reading Tasks

Your Name: _____ Partner: _____

The Ins and Outs of Doors (cont.)

First — Silently read "The Ins and Outs of Doors." You might see words you do not know. There might be parts you do not understand. Keep reading! Try to find out what the story is mainly about.

Then — Sum up the story. Write the main actions and most important information. If someone reads your summary, that person should know it is this story you are writing about.

_____
_____
_____
_____

After That — Read the story again. Use a pencil to circle or mark words you don't know. Note places that confuse you. Underline the main action or idea of each paragraph.

Next — Meet with your partner. Working together, decide which of these sets of doors are **adjacent**. Use your pencil to shade in the doors that are adjacent.

a. Which part or words from the story helped you pick the adjacent doors.
_____
_____

b. Still working with your partner, find the part of the story where the writer says he goes looking for an **alternate** door. When the writer is looking for an alternate door, is the writer looking for an adjacent door or a different door?
_____

Which part or words from the story helped you know?
_____
_____

©Teacher Created Resources   53   #2691 Close Reading with Text-Dependent Questions

UNIT 12

Text-Dependent Questions

Your Name: _____

The Ins and Outs of Doors (cont.)

Now Answer the story questions below.

1. How did the writer hurt herself the second time? Answer on the lines. In the box, draw a picture that illustrates how she did this.

   _____

   _____

   _____

2. At the beginning of the story, what is the writer's opinion about reading?

   _____

   Find and write down the sentence in the story that gives you the first hint that the author's opinion is going to change.

   _____

   _____

3. The last line of the passage uses the expression "on the contrary." Reread the last part of the passage. If a person says "on the contrary," does that person feel the same or the opposite?

   _____

   Which parts of the passage help you know?

   _____

   _____

4. Use evidence from the story to prove that reading is not a waste of time.

   _____

   _____

   _____

   _____

UNIT **12**

More TDQs

Your Name: _____

The Ins and Outs of Doors (cont.)

Then — Reread the entire story one last time. Think about who is writing the story and why.

5. If you told the writer that you didn't want to learn how to read, what do you think she would tell you?

_____
_____

6. To get her message across, the narrator of the story used the example of doors marked "Enter" and "Exit." The writer could have used different examples. Choose one of the following. Circle your choice. What might happen to the author because she couldn't read these signs? How might she get hurt or get herself in trouble?

CLOSED and **OPEN**   **ON** and **OFF**   **HOT** and **COLD**

_____
_____
_____
_____

7. In the last paragraph, the writer says, "You can imagine how crazy everything got." Then the writer says, "One firefighter said to me, 'Can't you read?'" Write at least three sentences that could go **in between** those two lines. Use your imagination when you describe the action! Read your lines to the class. Did they like what you imagined?

You can imagine how crazy everything got.
_____
_____
_____
_____
One firefighter said to me, "Can't you read?"

Learn More — Look up in a book or on the Internet an image of a "revolving door." See what they look like. Find out why they are good for the environment.

©Teacher Created Resources   55   #2691 Close Reading with Text-Dependent Questions

Shooting Fish

 The salmon could go no farther. A dam had been built. The dam was a barrier the salmon could not get past. It was too high to jump over. The salmon needed to go up the river. The fish had to return to the place where it had been born. Something had to happen if the salmon was going to complete its migration.

 Not all fish migrate, but salmon do. Salmon hatch out of eggs. Next, they migrate down to the ocean. They get big and strong. When they are adults, they complete their migration. They swim back to their spawning grounds. Somehow they know exactly where their spawning grounds are. They know what river they need to go up. They lay their eggs close to where they once hatched out.

 Dams are important. They help farmers have water for their crops. They are used to make electricity. They help stop flooding. They are important, but fish are important, too. People tried to help salmon by building fish ladders. Instead of one big leap, the salmon had to make lots of little leaps. People also tried catching salmon and taking them past the dams.

 Then someone thought of a salmon cannon. It cost less than making a fish ladder. It also meant that the salmon weren't exhausted. They didn't have to use up all their energy leaping up steps. They spent less time out of the water than when they were trapped and carried.

 Using water flow, the fish are sucked into a transport tube. The fish are in the tube for only five to ten seconds. During that time, they are misted so they don't dry out. The tube bends. It is long enough to go over a dam. The fish come shooting out the end! They can safely land in water just a few feet deep. The salmon cannon idea came from picking fruit! The cannon was first made to transport ripe fruit without bruising it!

UNIT **13**

Close-Reading Tasks

Your Name: _____ Partner: _____

Shooting Fish (cont.)

First — Silently read "Shooting Fish." You might see words you do not know. There might be parts you do not understand. Keep reading! Try to find out what the story is mainly about.

Then — Sum up the story. Write the main actions and most important information. If someone reads your summary, that person should know it is this story you are writing about.

_____
_____
_____
_____
_____
_____

After That — Read the story again. Use a pencil to circle or mark words you don't know. Note places that confuse you. Underline the main action or idea of each paragraph.

Next — Meet with your partner. Help each other find these words and terms in the text.

    barrier   spawning ground   exhausted   transport

Read the sentences around the words. Think about how they fit in the whole story. Write what the words mean. Which information in the text helps you figure out the meaning of the new words? The first row of the chart is done for you.

Word(s)	What It Means	Information That Helps
barrier	something that blocks your way	A dam was a barrier that stopped the salmon.
spawning ground		
exhausted		
transport		

©Teacher Created Resources   #2691 Close Reading with Text-Dependent Questions

UNIT **13**

Text-Dependent Questions

Your Name: _____

Shooting Fish (cont.)

Now Answer the story questions below.

1. Why are dams important? Using information from the story, give three reasons.

   _____
   _____
   _____

2. Fill in the stages of a salmon's migration.

   Stage 1: _Eggs hatch from the spawning ground._____

   Stage 2: _____
   _____

   Stage 3: _____
   _____

   Stage 4: _____
   _____

3. If a salmon is shot out of a salmon cannon and lands in water 10 feet deep, is the water deep enough for it to land safely? Use evidence from the story to defend your answer.

   _____
   _____

4. One could trap the salmon and carry them over the dam. Or, one could use a salmon cannon. Which one is better for the salmon? In your answer, quote the amount of time salmon spend out of the water when a salmon cannon is used.

   _____
   _____
   _____

#2691 Close Reading with Text-Dependent Questions 58 ©Teacher Created Resources

UNIT 13 — More TDQs

Your Name: _____

Shooting Fish (cont.)

Then — Reread the entire story one last time. As you read, think about how the story has a problem and a solution.

5. The first paragraph describes a problem. What is the problem?

   _____

   _____

6. Three solutions are given. What are the three solutions?

   _____

   _____

   _____

   Of these three solutions, which one does the author seem to think is the best? What makes you think so?

   _____

   _____

7. Reread the last two sentences of the story. When you were reading this story for the first time, did you ever think you would read about picking fruit? Explain.

   _____

   _____

   What big lesson do you think the author was trying to teach you about ideas and inventions when she included the last two lines?

   _____

   _____

Learn More — Use books or the Internet to find out more about salmon and their migration. On the back of this paper, write three sentences about what you learn. If you want, you can find pictures of the salmon cannon, fish ladders, and bears catching salmon as they return to their spawning grounds.

©Teacher Created Resources

Carrie the Carrier

1. "That terrier is nothing but a carrier! She's as useful as a barrel with a hole in it!" muttered Mr. Dang. Scowling, Mr. Dang pulled his slipper from the dog's mouth. "What is it with you and carrying things?" Mr. Dang asked the dog. "Do all terriers act this way, or is it just you? I could understand if you were collecting bones, but you pick up anything!"

2. "She's a real menace," Mrs. Dang said. She had overheard what Mr. Dang had said, and she wanted to add her two cents. "She's dangerous because you never know what she is going to pick up. Just the other day, she picked up my phone! She slobbered all over it! When I pulled it out of her mouth, it was all slimy and wet."

3. "Everything you put down is at risk," Viet agreed. "The other day, I couldn't find my backpack. Carrie had carried it outside. It wasn't even on the floor! I had put it on the bench, and she took it off the bench! Yes, that dog is a real menace. I think we should find her a new home."

4. Everyone was in agreement with Viet except Trang. "No," Trang objected. "Carrie is the best dog in the world. I taught her to carry my dolls for me. She is smart and well-trained." Trang's parents and brother didn't agree. They said a smart dog would know the difference between a doll, a slipper, a phone, and a backpack.

5. The next day, all the fire alarms went off. The sound was deafening. Smoke poured out of the neighbor's apartment. Everyone in the building ran outside. Then Ellen, the neighbor, started screaming. She had grabbed the wrong basket! She didn't have the basket with her three little kittens! Just then, Trang saw Carrie. Carrie was coming out Ellen's door. Carrie was carefully carrying a basket with three little whiskered faces poking out of it.

UNIT **14**

Close-Reading Tasks

Your Name: _____ Partner: _____

Carrie the Carrier (cont.)

First — Silently read "Carrie the Carrier." You might see words you do not know. There might be parts you do not understand. Keep reading! Try to find out what the story is mainly about.

Then — Sum up <u>paragraphs 1–4 only</u>. Write the main actions and most important information. If someone reads your summary, that person should know it is this story you are writing about, not a different story!

_____

_____

_____

_____

_____

After That — Read the story again. Use a pencil to circle or mark words you don't know. Note places that confuse you. Underline the main action or idea of each paragraph.

Next — Meet with your partner. Help each other find these words in the text.

    menace   slobbered   objected

Read the sentences around the words. Think about how they fit in the whole story. Decide what the words mean. Then answer the questions.

   a. Why is a lion in your back yard more likely to be a **menace** than a kitten?

       _____

       _____

   b. Why is a pencil no one has **slobbered** on better than one that has slobber on it?

       _____

       _____

   c. Why would parents **object** to their children eating nothing but ice cream all day?

       _____

       _____

©Teacher Created Resources

UNIT **14**

Text-Dependent Questions

Your Name: _____

Carrie the Carrier (cont.)

Now Answer the story questions below.

1. Why did Mr. and Mrs. Dang and Viet think Carrie wasn't very smart?

   _____

   _____

2. In the story, it says that Mrs. Dang wanted to "add her two cents." What does this mean? Did she want to give money to Mr. Dang?

   _____

   _____

   How do you know you are right? What happens in the story that shows you are right?

   _____

   _____

3. What mistake did Ellen make?

   _____

   Why might it be easy to make a mistake when there is smoke and fire alarms going off?

   _____

4. At the end of the passage, what is Carrie carrying in the basket? Write your answer on the lines below. In the box on the right, draw a picture that shows your answer.

   _____

   _____

   Even though the story doesn't exactly tell you what Carrie is carrying in the basket, you were able to use clues to understand this information. What clues at the end of the passage help you understand exactly what is in the basket?

   _____

   _____

UNIT 14

More TDQs

Your Name: _____

Carrie the Carrier (cont.)

Then — Reread the entire story one last time. As you read, think about how the story has a problem and a solution.

5. In just one or two sentences, sum up what happens in paragraph 5 of the passage.

    _____

    _____

    _____

6. Earlier in the story, you're told that Mr. and Mrs. Dang and Viet agree that Carrie should be put in a new home. Do you think they still felt the same way after what happened in paragraph 5? Tell why or why not.

    _____

    _____

7. What did each of these characters say in the early part of the story that would make the reader think Carrie might go to a new home?

    Mr. Dang: _____

    Mrs. Dang: _____

    Viet: _____

    Why do you think the author made sure you knew what Mr. and Mrs. Dang and Viet felt about Carrie before you read the last paragraph?

    _____

    _____

Learn More — Find out where some of the smoke detectors in your school are. On the back of this paper, make a map or use words to describe where one of the smoke detectors is. Make sure your map or description is accurate enough to pinpoint exactly where the one smoke detector you are writing about is located.

©Teacher Created Resources   63   #2691 Close Reading with Text-Dependent Questions

Never Growing Old

 Try picking up something that weighs four pounds. (Your reading book weighs less than four pounds, but you could use that.) Put it in your right hand. Hold your hand straight up in the air. Maintain this position for 10 or more minutes. If you try this, you will know it is hard to do. It's even difficult if your hand is empty!

 Carroll Spinney holds his hand that way for his job. Spinney is a puppeteer. He is the man in the Big Bird suit. Big Bird is a character on *Sesame Street*. *Sesame Street* is a television show for children. Big Bird is bright yellow. He is eight feet and two inches tall. Spinney's hand is holding up Big Bird's head. Spinney's own head is in Big Birds neck.

 There are no eyeholes in Big Bird's costume, so how does Spinney see? Spinney has a small monitor. The tiny screen is attached to his chest. Spinney can see a video of himself acting on the screen. If there is no video feed, a small hole is made in the costume. In those cases, Big Bird wears a necktie. The necktie covers up the hole.

 Big Bird is six years old on the show. He never grows older. The truth is that Big Bird grew younger! When the show was first written, Big Bird was a goofy adult. Big Bird often misunderstands words. In one show, he said the alphabet as one long word! After saying the 26 letters, he wondered what the long word meant. Big Bird said, "If I ever find out just what this word can mean, I'll be the smartest bird the world has ever seen."

 Spinney plays another character on the show, too. He is also Oscar the Grouch. Oscar lives in a garbage can. Oscar's costume is green, but in the first shows, it was orange. Oscar became green after he went on vacation to Swamp Mushy Muddy.

UNIT 15

Close-Reading Tasks

Your Name: _____   Partner: _____

Never Growing Old (cont.)

First — Silently read "Never Growing Old." You might see words you do not know. There might be parts you do not understand. Keep reading! Try to find out what the story is mainly about.

Then — Sum up paragraphs 2–5 only. Write the main actions and most important information. If someone reads your summary, that person should know it is this story you are writing about, not a different story!

_____

_____

_____

_____

After That — Read the story again. Use a pencil to circle or mark words you don't know. Note places that confuse you. Underline the main action or idea of each paragraph.

Next — Meet with your partner. Help each other find these words in the text.

   maintain   character   costume   misunderstands

Read the sentences around the words. Think about how they fit in the whole story. Tell each other what you think the words mean.

Then think about how the prefix *mis* changed the meaning of the word *understand*. The prefix *mis* means "mistaken, wrong, or bad." Write *mis* in front of the words. Then write down what the words mean.

  a. __mis__ *understand* means ___not understand correctly___

  b. _____ *name* means _____

  c. _____ *count* means _____

  d. _____ *lead* means _____

  e. _____ *behave* means _____

  f. _____ *use* means _____

  g. _____ *fortune* means _____

©Teacher Created Resources   #2691 Close Reading with Text-Dependent Questions

UNIT **15**

Text-Dependent Questions

Your Name: _____

Never Growing Old (cont.)

Now Answer the story questions below.

1. How did Big Bird's age change over time? Explain. _____
   _____

2. Is Big Bird's age still changing? Circle your answer.   **Yes**   **No**

   Then write down the sentence from the story that gives the answer.
   _____

3. Think about how Spinney fits inside Big Bird's costume. Show the following things on the drawing:

   • Show where Spinney's head goes. Draw a head in that place.

   • Show where Spinney's right hand goes. Draw a hand in that place.

   Write down the words or sentences from the story that prove you are correct.

   Head: _____
   _____
   _____

   Right hand: _____
   _____
   _____

   Big Bird's head
   Big Bird's neck
   Big Bird's chest
   Big Bird's waist
   Big Bird's legs
   Big Bird's feet

4. Is Big Bird the only character on the show that changed? Defend your answer with evidence from the story.
   _____
   _____
   _____

#2691 Close Reading with Text-Dependent Questions

UNIT **15**

More TDQs

Your Name: _____

Never Growing Old (cont.)

Then Reread the entire story one last time. Think about paragraph 1 and how it starts the story.

5. Write a very short summary of paragraph 1. What happens in this part of the passage?

   _____

   _____

6. If a person has read only the title and the first paragraph, what might that person think this story will be about? Why?

   _____

   _____

   Why does the story start this way? What does it tell you about puppeteers?

   _____

   _____

7. Reread Big Bird's quote at the end of paragraph 4. Do you think this quote of Big Bird's helped you understand Big Bird's character? Tell why or why not.

   _____

   _____

Big Bird wishes he knew the meaning of the word *abcdefghijklmnopqrstuvwxyz*. What could it mean? Make up a meaning that sounds about right to you. (You are making up the meaning, so you cannot be wrong! However, your meaning should not be mean or nasty.)

The word *abcdefghijklmnopqrstuvwxyz* means "_____."

And since this word now means something, use it in a sentence.

_____

_____

Learn More Think of another puppet or fictional character. Find out three facts about the puppet or character. Write this information on the back of this paper.

©Teacher Created Resources   67   #2691 Close Reading with Text-Dependent Questions

Always First

1. Sam was first in line for ice cream. "I'm older," he said to Laura, "and it's age before beauty." Laura sighed. Sam always said that. Saying it made grown-ups smile. Laura knew Sam didn't really mean it. Sam didn't care what anyone looked like. He just wanted to be first in line.

2. When Laura was younger, Sam would say to her, "You can be first in line when you are my age. You just have to patient." When Laura got older, she realized she was being tricked. It didn't matter how patient she was. She would never get to Sam's age! He would always be two years older!

3. After the ice cream, their grandfather told them they had time to go to two more exhibits at the zoo. Sam said he would go first so they could end on what Laura wanted. Laura just sighed when her smiling grandfather told Sam he was proud of having such a polite and thoughtful grandson.

4. Sam chose the giraffe exhibit. There, for a dollar extra, one could buy some carrots to feed the giraffes. Once again, Sam went first. Then when Laura went to buy her carrots, she was told, "Sorry. The zoo is now closing. That boy in front of you got the last giraffe treat. Come back tomorrow if you want to feed the giraffes." Of course, Sam had finished feeding the giraffe before Laura could ask him to share.

5. Laura practiced a speech inside her head on the way home. Laura said her speech at dinner. She was clear. Her voice was firm and didn't wobble or shake. She gave a good solid reason as to why Sam and she should take turns being first. Sam's parents agreed with Sam when Sam pointed out that age came before beauty. "Yes," they agreed, "and that's why you will be taking out the garbage from now on. You're old enough to start doing more work around here."

UNIT 16 | Close-Reading Tasks

Your Name: _____   Partner: _____

Always First (cont.)

First — Silently read "Always First." You might see words you do not know. There might be parts you do not understand. Keep reading! Try to find out what the story is mainly about.

Then — Sum up paragraphs 1–4 only. Write the main actions and most important information. If someone reads your summary, that person should know it is this story you are writing about, not a different story!

_____

_____

_____

_____

After That — Read the story again. Use a pencil to circle or mark words you don't know. Note places that confuse you. Underline the main action or idea of each paragraph.

Next — Meet with your partner. Help each other find these new words in the text.

       patient   exhibit   polite   firm

Read the sentences around the words. Think about how they fit in the whole story. Write what the words mean. Which information in the text helps you and your partner figure out the meaning of the new words? The first row of the chart is done for you.

Word	What It Means	Information That Helps
patient	easygoing, willing to not rush or get upset	Even if Laura was patient, she would never be the same age as Sam.
exhibit		
polite		
firm		

©Teacher Created Resources   69   #2691 Close Reading with Text-Dependent Questions

UNIT **16**

Text-Dependent Questions

Your Name: _____

Always First (cont.)

Now Answer the story questions below.

1. Why didn't Laura get to feed the giraffe? Use information from the story to give two reasons.

   _____

   _____

2. Is there a chance that Laura didn't get to see the last exhibit she wanted to see? Explain.

   _____

   _____

   Write down one sentence from the story that helped you answer the question.

   _____

3. What does the saying "age before beauty" mean?

   _____

   _____

   An older lady and a young pretty princess help at a shoe store. According to Sam, which one should be helped first? In the box, draw a picture to show your answer. On the lines, explain why you gave this answer.

   _____

   _____

   _____

   _____

4. Laura is 7 years old. Sam is 9. In two years, will Laura be the same age as Sam? Explain.

   _____

   _____

UNIT **16**

Your Name: _____

Always First (cont.)

Then — Reread the entire story one last time.

5. Sum up the last paragraph. What happens in this part of the story?

_____

_____

6. In the earlier paragraphs, what happens when Sam says "age before beauty"? Give at least one specific example.

_____

_____

_____

How is this different from what happens after he says "age before beauty" in paragraph 5?

_____

_____

_____

7. There is an illustration (drawing) that goes with the passage. How does this drawing illustrate (show) the meaning of the passage's final sentences?

_____

_____

_____

Learn More — *Etiquette* is the word we use for polite social behavior. In our society, it is proper etiquette to provide a seat or open a door to an adult who is older than you. Research or think of three etiquette rules when it comes to eating.

Rule #1: _____

Rule #2: _____

Rule #3: _____

Sportsmanship

No one thought it was possible. No one thought it could be done. No one thought the human body was capable of it. Then on May 6, 1954, it was done. The impossible had become possible. Someone broke the four-minute mile. The man was Roger Bannister. His time was 3 minutes and 59.4 seconds. That is all it took him to run one mile.

The second man to run a sub-four-minute mile was John Landy. Landy's time was one and a half seconds faster than Bannister's. It was 3 minutes and 57.9 seconds. It took only 46 days for Landy to break Bannister's record. Landy held on to his record for over three years. Landy was fast, but he is known for more than his speed. He is also known for his sportsmanship.

The year was 1956. Landy was in a race. It was an important race. It was for the National Championships. A man named Ron Clarke was also in the race. The runners were on their third lap. Then something happened. A runner clipped Clarke's heel. This made Clarke fall down. Landy was close behind Clarke. Landy didn't want to hit Clarke so he leapt over him. He didn't leap far enough.

All the track runners had spikes on their shoes. The spikes were like little nails. The spikes helped stop the runners from slipping. Landy scraped one of Clarke's shoulders with his spikes. Landy could have kept running. He had done nothing wrong. After all, falls are part of racing.

Landy stopped. He turned back! He checked on Clarke. All the other runners kept running. They got far ahead. When Landy knew Clarke was okay, he started running again. No one thought he would. Why would he when he was so far behind? Landy didn't quit. Instead, he ran. He caught up with the other runners in the last two laps! He won the race! Landy's catching up is thought to be one of the greatest moments in the history of sports. So is his act of sportsmanship.

UNIT 17 — Close-Reading Tasks

Sportsmanship (cont.)

First — Silently read "Sportsmanship." You might see words you do not know. There might be parts you do not understand. Keep reading! Try to find out what the story is mainly about.

Then — Sum up paragraphs 2–5 only. Write the main actions and most important information. If someone reads your summary, that person should know it is this story you are writing about, not a different story!

_____

-

_____

After That — Read the story again. Use a pencil to circle or mark words you don't know. Note places that confuse you. Underline the main action or idea of each paragraph.

Next — Meet with your partner. Help each other find these words in the text.

    capable   record   clipped   spikes

Read the sentences around the words. Think about how they fit in the whole story. Write what the words mean. Which information in the text helps you and your partner define (give the meaning of) the words. One row of the chart is filled in for you.

Word	What It Means	Information That Helps
capable		
record		
clipped	to hit with a slight blow	A runner clipped Clarke's heel and made him fall.
spikes		

©Teacher Created Resources   #2691 Close Reading with Text-Dependent Questions

UNIT **17**

Text-Dependent Questions

Your Name: _____

Sportsmanship (cont.)

Now Answer the story questions below.

1. What made Landy stop running in the 1956 National Championships race?

   _____
   _____

2. Why do runners have spikes on their shoes? Write down the sentence from the story that tells you the answer. Remember to put quotation marks (" ") around the sentence.

   _____

3. The second paragraph starts with this sentence: "The second man to run a sub-four-minute mile was John Landy."

   a. What does "sub-four-minute" mean in this sentence?

   _____

   How do you know? Use evidence from the story to prove your answer.

   _____
   _____

   b. Now use what you know to say if *a subway* is more likely to go above the ground or underground. Why?

   _____
   _____

4. Who held the record longer for breaking the four-minute mile? Check the box beside your choice.

   ❏ Bannister
   ❏ Landy

   Use evidence from the story to support your answer.

   _____
   _____

   Challenge: Landy broke Bannister's record in 1954. In what month of that year did he break it? You must use information from the story to figure this out.

   _____

UNIT 17

More TDQs

Your Name: _____

Sportsmanship (cont.)

Then Reread the entire story one last time. Think about how paragraph 1 relates to the rest of the story.

5. Sum up paragraph 1. What happens in this part of the story?

   _____

   _____

6. Why do you think the author began the story this way? How did it help you understand more about what kind of runner Landy was?

   _____

   _____

7. Write a new beginning for the story. Your beginning should be the thoughts inside Landy's head when he breaks Bannister's record. Will your version of Landy be happy, tired, or worried? It is up to you! Write at least three sentences. Remember to use the word "I," since you will be writing as if you were Landy.

   _____

   _____

   _____

   _____

   _____

   How does your new beginning change the passage? Do you think it is a better beginning? Is the main idea still the same?

   _____

   _____

Learn More Find out two facts about Landy or Bannister. On the back of this paper, write the facts in sentence form and share them with the class.

On the Leash

1. Pets should be kept on leashes. Pets are safer when they are leashed. They are less likely to get lost or hurt. They are less likely to get in fights with other pets.

2. Just yesterday, I took my pet to the park. I had to go in front and pull on the leash. I kept the leash taut and never let it sag or droop. My pet was going at a snail's pace, and I had to strain against the rope. Pulling the rope tight was the only way to get him to pick up his pace and go faster.

3. At the park, my pet got loose. Somehow the leash had gotten tangled on a pole. My pet broke free. I couldn't get the leash loose. This happens just a bit too often for me. Unfortunately, the only way to get my pet to come back is to make a lot of noise. My pet gets upset of course, but he is the one who chooses to run away in the first place.

4. Yesterday, my pet was in danger! Five bigger pets had gotten loose and were chasing him! My pet had to climb a high, steep ladder. The other pets were right behind him! My pet couldn't go back the way he had come. My pet had to slip down a steep metal hill to get away. The whole time he was coming down, I was afraid he was going to get hurt even though he was smiling and laughing. Then he ran back to the ladder and climbed up again!

5. My pet wanted to go home after that, and I was glad. It was so hot, it felt like we were in a blazing fire. I was panting by the time we got back home. I had to pant, because I needed to cool off. My silly pet thinks I'm panting because I'm tired. He doesn't know I release extra heat by panting. That's how dogs cool down.

UNIT **18**

Close-Reading Tasks

Your Name: _____   Partner: _____

On the Leash (cont.)

First — Silently read "On the Leash." You might see words you do not know. There might be parts you do not understand. Keep reading! Try to find out what the story is mainly about.

Then — Sum up the story. Write the main actions and most important information. If someone reads your summary, that person should know it is this story you are writing about.

_____
_____
_____
_____
_____

After That — Read the story again. Use a pencil to circle or mark words you don't know. Note places that confuse you. Underline the main action or idea of each paragraph.

Next — Meet with your partner. Help each other find these words in the text.

taut   sag   pace   release

Read the sentences around the words. Think about how they fit in the whole story. Think about what the words must mean. Use that information to answer the questions. Circle **is** or **is not** to make the sentence correct. Then tell how the story helps you know this information. The first one is done for you.

a. When something is **sagging**, it   (**is**)   **is not**   drooping. I know this because
   the story says the leash wasn't sagging or drooping.

b. When something is pulled **taut**, it   **is**   **is not**   sagging. I know this because
   _____

c. One's **pace**   **is**   **is not**   the speed one is walking or going. I know this because
   _____

d. When something is **released**, it   **is**   **is not**   let go. I know this because
   _____

©Teacher Created Resources

UNIT **18**

Text-Dependent Questions

Your Name: _____

On the Leash (cont.)

Now Answer the story questions below.

1. Find the sentence in the story where it tells what the narrator does to get his pet to come back when his pet gets away. Using only words from the sentence, tell what the narrator does. (**Hint:** The narrator is the one telling the story.)

   The narrator _____ to get his pet to come back.

   How do you think the narrator did this? What was the narrator probably doing?

   _____

   _____

2. What reasons does the narrator give for keeping pets on leashes? Name three reasons.

   Reason #1: _____

   Reason #2: _____

   Reason #3: _____

3. The narrator says that his pet was going "at a snail's pace." What does this expression mean in the way it is used here?

   _____

   Which parts of the story helped you know what the narrator meant when he used the expression "at a snail's pace"?

   _____

   _____

4. Look back at paragraph 4. What is the "pet" really doing in this paragraph? What piece of playground equipment is he using? In the box, draw a picture of the playground equipment. On the lines, show how you know this from the clues given in the story.

_____

_____

_____

#2691 Close Reading with Text-Dependent Questions ©Teacher Created Resources

UNIT 18

More TDQs

Your Name: _____

On the Leash (cont.)

Then   Reread the entire story one last time. Think about what you learn in the last paragraph.

5. What do you learn about the narrator in the last paragraph? How do you learn it?

_____
_____
_____

6. Why do you think the author waited until the end to let you know the narrator is a dog?

_____
_____

When you reread the story the last time, was it easier to notice the parts that hinted that the narrator might be a dog? Write down two places where it hinted that a dog was narrating.

_____
_____

7. Write a new beginning for the story. Your beginning should be one or two sentences. In your new beginning, tell that you are a dog.

_____
_____
_____

Do you think the story is better with the new beginning? Why or why not?

_____
_____

Learn More   Different states have different laws when it comes to pets and dogs. Call your local government office or look on its website and find out two laws about pets. If you want, type "silly pet laws" into an Internet search engine. Think about why some of these laws were written. Then, on the back of this paper, write a pet law that is not silly.

©Teacher Created Resources   79   #2691 Close Reading with Text-Dependent Questions

Surviving the Fire

 Flames roared. The fire blazed for days. Trees burned. The ground became covered in ash. The fire had been set on purpose. Researchers were studying what the fire did to plants and animals. After the fire, scientists saw some animals. The animals were strange looking. They had lots of spines. They had long snouts. The researchers saw many of these animals roaming around in places full of ashes. One scientist said, "Their noses are always in the ashes. They didn't seem to care at all."

 The animals were echidnas. They live in Australia. They are mammals. Most mammals give birth to live young. Echidnas don't. They lay eggs. How did the echidnas survive the fire? Why were there so many roaming about? Why were their snouts in the ashes? The scientists wanted to know.

echidna

 Before the fire, researchers had trapped some of the echidnas. They put trackers on them. The trackers let the scientists know where the echidnas went. The trackers also let them know what state the echidnas were in. Echidnas could go into torpor. Torpor is a state in which the body slows down. The animal barely breathes. It stays very still. When an animal is in torpor, little energy is used. The animal does not need to drink or eat.

 During the fire, the echidnas hid. They stayed in the cool ground. They hid inside thick tree trunks. Safe, away from the flames, they went into torpor. They went into torpor after the fire, too! Over and over, they slipped into torpor. Sometimes they were in torpor for four days! This lasted for weeks.

 After a fire, the ground has been blackened. It takes time for it to become green. Seeds need to sprout. Plants need to grow. Insects need to hatch out of eggs. The echidna roams, looking for food. If it can't find enough, it goes back into torpor. It survives by waiting.

UNIT 19

Close-Reading Tasks

Your Name: _____ Partner: _____

Surviving the Fire (cont.)

First — Silently read "Surviving the Fire." You might see words you do not know. There might be parts you do not understand. Keep reading! Try to find out what the story is mainly about.

Then — Sum up the story. Write the main actions and most important information. If someone reads your summary, that person should know it is this story you are writing about.

_____

_____

_____

_____

_____

After That — Read the story again. Use a pencil to circle or mark words you don't know. Note places that confuse you. Underline the main action or idea of each paragraph.

Next — Meet with your partner. Help each other find these words in the text.

    researcher   roaming   snouts   torpor

Read the sentences around the words. Think about how they fit in the whole story. Then draw lines to match each word to its definition. The first one is done for you.

researcher	a state where everything is slowed down
roaming	moving about
snouts	noses
torpor	one who studies something, a scientist

(researcher is matched to "one who studies something, a scientist")

Then pick one word. Use information from the story to prove to that your word is matched correctly. Your partner should pick a different word.

My word is _____. It is correctly matched, because in the story

_____

My partner's word is _____. It is correctly matched, because

_____

©Teacher Created Resources

UNIT **19**

Text-Dependent Questions

Your Name: _____

Surviving the Fire *(cont.)*

Now Answer the story questions below.

1. How did the researchers know where the echidnas were going?

   _____
   _____

2. Why might an echidna need to go into a state of torpor a couple of weeks after a fire? Your answer should come from the information given in the story.

   _____
   _____

3. If an echidna no longer needs to go into torpor, what has happened to the blackened areas? On the lines, write at least two things that have happened to the blackened area to make it okay for an echidna to come out of torpor. In the box, draw a picture of what the blackened area now looks like.

   _____
   _____
   _____
   _____
   _____

4. What makes echidnas different from most mammals? Find and quote the **three** sentences in the story that give you the answer.

   _____
   _____
   _____
   _____

UNIT **19**

More TDQs

Your Name: _____

Surviving the Fire (cont.)

Then — Reread the entire story one last time. Think about what you learn in the last paragraph.

5. In one or two sentences, tell what the first paragraph is mainly about. If you have not yet been told the name of an animal, you should not use that word!

   _____

   _____

6. Is this story fiction or nonfiction? Check the box beside the correct choice, and then answer the questions below.

   ❏ fiction
   ❏ nonfiction

   a. How do you know if the story is fiction or nonfiction?

   _____

   _____

   b. What if the first sentence of the story went like this: *The mammal who laid an egg didn't move for four days.* Why might someone think this was the start of a fiction story?

   _____

   _____

   c. Write two sentences that could follow this sentence that would help the reader know the story is nonfiction.

   The mammal who laid an egg didn't move for four days. _____

   _____

   _____

7. Many small animals will go into states of torpor at night or when it is very cold. Think like a scientist and write why this might happen.

   _____

   _____

Learn More — Look in books or on the Internet to find out three different facts about echidnas. On the back of this paper, write them in sentence form. Read them to your class.

Cat for Dessert

1. Jane's Dad was really irritated! Angrily, he said, "Get that cat out of the house! Look how it has shredded the furniture with its sharp claws. We'll have to re-cover this chair and couch. It's torn the fabric to pieces!"

2. The cat belonged to Jane's Uncle Bruce. Uncle Bruce was Jane's favorite uncle. He was always teasing her. Jane's dad told Jane that when they were little, Uncle Bruce was known for joking around. Uncle Bruce apologized. After saying he was sorry, he told Jane's dad he would get the torn cloth replaced. "And," he said with a funny gleam in his eye, "I'll put the cat to good use."

3. Uncle Bruce cooked dinner that night for everyone. He said it was the least he could do. The meal was delicious. It was pizza. Jane had never had homemade pizza before. She ate six slices! "Better leave room for dessert," Uncle Bruce told her. "You're not going to want to miss it."

4. Jane's dad asked what it was. "Cat," Uncle Bruce said, rising from his chair. "I'll get it right now. We're having the cat for dessert. I told you I'd make good use of it." There was a terrible silence. As Uncle Bruce went into the kitchen, everyone stared at each other fearfully. What had he done?

5. Uncle Bruce returned to the dining room carefully carrying a flat pan above his head. When he set it down, people gasped. Uncle Bruce had baked a cat. The "cat" was a cat-shaped cake! It was frosted with brown frosting. It had gum drops for eyes and black licorice whiskers. Jane's father laughed loudly. "Don't ever change, little brother," he said. "Don't ever change."

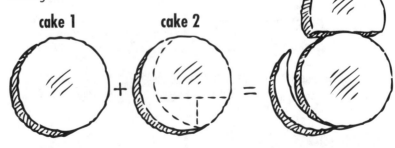

UNIT 20　　　　　　　　　　　　　　　　　　　　　　　　　　　Close-Reading Tasks

Your Name: _____　Partner: _____

Cat for Dessert (cont.)

First — Silently read "Cat for Dessert." You might see words you do not know. There might be parts you do not understand. Keep reading! Try to find out what the story is mainly about.

Then — Sum up the story. Write the main actions and most important information. If someone reads your summary, that person should know it is this story you are writing about.

_____

_____

_____

_____

_____

After That — Read the story again. Use a pencil to circle or mark words you don't know. Note places that confuse you. Underline the main action or idea of each paragraph.

Next — Meet with your partner. Help each other find these words in the text.

　　　irritated　　　shredded　　　fabric　　　apologized

Read the sentences around the words. Think about what the words must mean. Use that information to find synonyms for the words in the story. A **synonym** is a word or phrase that means exactly or nearly the same thing as another word or phrase.
Remember: Your synonym must be a word or phrase from the story!

Word	Synonym (Word or Phrase)
irritated	
shredded	
fabric	
apologized	

©Teacher Created Resources　　　　　　　#2691 Close Reading with Text-Dependent Questions

UNIT 20

Text-Dependent Questions

Your Name: _____

Cat for Dessert (cont.)

Now Answer the story questions below.

1. How do you know Jane's dad is not angry with his brother at the end of the story? Quote something Jane's dad says as part of your answer.

   _____
   _____
   _____

2. What did the cat Uncle Bruce baked look like? Write down three facts.

   _____
   _____
   _____
   _____

3. What did Uncle Bruce say that made people worry that he might have really made his cat into dessert?

   _____
   _____
   _____

4. It says in the story that Uncle Bruce had "a funny gleam in his eye." Does this mean Uncle Bruce had dirt in his eye, or does it mean that he had the beginning of an idea?

   _____
   _____

   How do you know? What parts of the story helped you find the answer?

   _____
   _____

UNIT **20**

More TDQs

Your Name: _____

Cat for Dessert (cont.)

Then | Reread the entire story one last time. Think about how the picture helps you understand how Uncle Bruce made his cat cake.

5. Tell how Uncle Bruce made the cat cake part of his dessert. Use the picture to help you.

   _____
   _____
   _____

6. Why do you think the author included this picture?

   _____
   _____

   Do you think having the picture made the story better? Why or why not?

   _____
   _____

7. In your opinion, is Uncle Bruce a good uncle? Tell why or why not. Give examples.

   _____
   _____
   _____

Learn More | Look in books, call a vet, or look on the Internet to find out why cats shred furniture. Then, with a gleam in your eye, think of a way to stop them! Write your idea below. Share what you learn and your idea with the class.

   _____
   _____
   _____

©Teacher Created Resources

The Mouse and the Tornado

 "Eek! Eek!" Mark's mother screeched. "A mouse! I see a mouse! It ran right over my foot! Mark's mother jumped onto a chair, and now she pointed with her finger. "There! It ran behind that pile of bags. Get it! Oh, please catch it and take it away from here!"

 Mark got a broom. He started to jab at the pile of bags. Nothing happened. Mark gave one more poke, and then the mouse darted out. The tiny creature ran across the room. It went into the living room. Mark's mother started to scream again. Mark's friend Carly was visiting. Carly put her hands over her ears. She thought Mark's mother's voice was worse than the mouse! "Her high-pitched screaming makes my skin crawl," Carly thought.

 "Help! Help! Tornado! Tornado!" screamed Mark's mother. Carly stared at Mark's mother with disbelief. Was Carly hearing correctly? Was Mark's mother really comparing a tiny little mouse to a tornado? Carly knew all about tornados.

 Tornados are spinning columns of air. They look like funnels, with the narrow end touching the ground. Sometimes they are called "twisters." The most powerful tornados have had wind speeds of more than 300 miles per hour! If a house is in its path, a tornado could knock over the house! It could suck up things and carry them far away.

 As Mark's mother continued to scream "Tornado!" over and over, Carly began to wonder if there really was a tornado. Mark ran to the window and looked out. When he shouted out that he saw it coming, Carly got really scared. Was the house going to be blown away? Were they all in danger? Mark rushed to the door and opened it. "Tornado!" Mark said, letting in a large cat. "There's a mouse in the house. Be a useful pet for once and find it for Mom!"

UNIT 21

Peer-Led Tasks

Your Name: _____

The Mouse and the Tornado (cont.)

For this activity, work in groups of four. If your group has fewer than four members, share the Mr./Ms. Future task. Begin by deciding who will perform each task.

Title	Student's Name	What Is Your Task?
Mr./Ms. Meaning		Explain the meaning of unfamiliar words.
Mr./Ms. Plot		Summarize what is happening in the passage.
Mr./Ms. Ask		Ask important questions about the passage.
Mr./Ms. Future		Guess what will happen next in the passage.

First Read paragraphs 1–2 of "The Mouse and the Tornado." Stop and do these tasks:

Mr./Ms. Meaning: Think about the words *screeched*, *jab*, and *poke*. Tell your group what they might mean.

Mr./Ms. Plot: Summarize what happened in paragraphs 1 and 2. Tell how knowing what *screeched*, *jab*, and *poke* mean helps you know what is going on.

Mr./Ms. Ask: Check to see if your group knows what is going on by asking one question about each character. (There are three characters.)

Mr./Ms. Future: Guess what is going to happen next. Will the mouse get caught? Will Carly help catch the mouse? Which parts of the story so far helped you answer?

Next Read paragraphs 1–4 of "The Mouse and the Tornado." Then do the following tasks:

Mr./Ms. Meaning: Think about the words *disbelief* and *funnels*. Define them for your group.

Mr./Ms. Plot: Remind the group what happened in paragraphs 1 and 2. Then sum up for your group what happened in paragraphs 3 and 4.

Mr./Ms. Ask: Ask two questions about paragraph 4. One question should be about tornados. The other question should be about how this paragraph is different from the other paragraphs.

Mr./Ms. Future: Use evidence from the passage to say what you think will happen next.

Finally Read the entire passage from start to finish. As a group, do the following:

- Discuss the ending of the story. Share your thoughts. Did you like it?
- Find and share quotes that make you think a real twister is coming!
- Discuss the author's purpose in writing this story. Do you think the author wanted you to feel scared, puzzled, and/or surprised? Did the author succeed? Tell why or why not.

Around the Cape

1. Doug saw the shark. It was 12 feet long. It was coming up out of the seaweed with its mouth open wide. Doug knew it was going to attack. Doug was a volunteer. He and two other men were donating their time for free. All three volunteers were trained divers wearing wet suits.

2. Doug shot at the shark. His spear hit the shark in its dorsal fin. The shark turned and bit the spear lodged in its back fin. It bent the spear in half before pulling it out. The shark swam off, but its blood had attracted other sharks. Lynne Cox hadn't seen the shark. All she knew was that when she turned and looked for Doug, she couldn't see him.

3. Cox was a long-distance swimmer. She was trying to be the first person to swim around the Cape of Good Hope. The Cape of Good Hope is at the tip of Africa. It is where the Atlantic and Indian Oceans meet. The water Cox was swimming in was very cold. It was only 58 degrees. The waves were strong and high. At the minimum, the swim would be 10 miles long. Cox knew she might have to swim a lot farther. It would depend on the currents. The currents might push her backward or out farther into the ocean.

4. Cox would not wear a wet suit. She would not coat her body with grease to help stay warm. She would not wear flippers or a mask. She would only wear a simple one-piece bathing suit. A boat would stay close, but no person or thing on the boat could touch her.

5. The waters around the cape were infested with sharks. Doug and the other volunteers helped keep Cox safe. They took turns watching for sharks while holding on to a rope attached to the boat. Cox finished her difficult and dangerous swim. She swam by herself, but her volunteers helped keep her safe.

UNIT **22**

Peer-Led Tasks

Your Name: _____

Around the Cape (cont.)

For this activity, work in groups of four. If your group has fewer than four members, share the Mr./Ms. Future task. Begin by deciding who will perform each task.

Title	Student's Name	What Is Your Task?
Mr./Ms. Meaning		Explain the meaning of unfamiliar words.
Mr./Ms. Plot		Summarize what is happening in the passage.
Mr./Ms. Ask		Ask important questions about the passage.
Mr./Ms. Future		Guess what will happen next in the passage.

First Read paragraphs 1 and 2 of "Around the Cape." Stop reading and do these tasks:

Mr./Ms. Meaning: Think about what the words *volunteer, donating, dorsal,* and *lodged* mean. Tell your group what you think.

Mr./Ms. Plot: Summarize what happened in paragraphs 1 and 2. Tell how knowing what *volunteer, donating, dorsal,* and *lodged* mean helps you know what is going on.

Mr./Ms. Ask: Check to see if your group knows what is going on by asking a question about Doug, the shark, and Lynne Cox.

Mr./Ms. Future: Guess what is going to happen next. What do you think will happen to Doug? Who is Cox? Does the title help you figure out what is going on?

Next Read paragraphs 1–4 of "Around the Cape." Then do the following tasks:

Mr./Ms. Meaning: Think about the words *minimum* and *grease*. Tell your group what they mean.

Mr./Ms. Plot: Remind the group of the events that happened in paragraphs 1–2. Then sum up paragraphs 3–4.

Mr./Ms. Ask: Ask a what/where/why/how question (one each) about Cox and her swim.

Mr./Ms. Future: Guess what will happen next. Do you think Cox will swim around the Cape? Do you think Doug will be safe? Use evidence from the story to tell why or why not.

Finally Read the entire passage from start to finish. As a group, do the following:

- Discuss the ending of the story. Did you like it? Does it make you want to be a long-distance swimmer? Do you admire Cox, or do you think she was taking too many risks?

- Find and share some quotes that make you see how dangerous Cox's swim was.

- Talk about the author's purpose in writing this story. What do you think the author wanted you to understand about the people and events in this story? Share your opinions.

- Take a vote: Who in your group would want to be one of Cox's volunteers? Who in your group would want to try and swim around the Cape of Good Hope?

Answer Key

"Dead-Tree Wishes" (pages 8–11)
Summary: A woodcutter gets two wishes for sparing a dead tree. He wishes his children were silent. Then he wishes his wish undone because their mouths are sealed.

Vocabulary: deed = "an act"; grant = "to give"; sealed = "closed tightly"

1. They make their homes in the holes.
2. Their lips were sealed. Answers will vary. Students should understand that a sealed mouth would mean that they couldn't talk, eat, or drink.
3. Students should draw one tree with nothing on it and another with many leaves. "There was not one speck of green on it. It did not have even the tiniest leaf!"
4. C; The children wish to be king (boy) and queen (girl).
5. "Once upon a time"; this tells you that you are about to read a fairy tale.
6. She makes you think the woodcutter might wish for something the children want or a beach house or a new car. Accept appropriate responses.
7. The last line tells you this information about the woodcutter's last wish.

"Going, Going, Gone!" (pages 12–15)
Summary: Little penguins on Middle Island were being killed by foxes who had been brought there. Special sheepdogs were brought in to help. The penguins were saved.

1. They crossed from the mainland when it was low tide.
2. Special sheepdogs from Italy were brought in to protect them.
3. Accept any picture that shows a small tunnel. Penguins can't fly.
4. Both work five days, with two days off. The dogs, however, work day and night.
5. It's about how the penguins will soon be gone because of the foxes.
7. paragraph 5; "The idea worked!" or "The dogs kept the penguins safe!"

"Helping Hands" (pages 16–19)
Summary: Darcy keeps asking her mom to carry her stuffed animals. Then she asks her mom to carry her. Her mom can't because she only has three hands.

Vocabulary: plead = "beg"; stern = "be firm"; appreciate = "be thankful or glad for"

1. First, she carried a stuffed lion in her left hand. Next, she carried a stuffed octopus in her right hand. Then, she carried a stuffed horse in her middle hand.
2. a ton; when Darcy's mom says, "I don't think a stuffed lion weighs 2,000 pounds."
3. It isn't possible, because it would be too heavy to carry.
4. She is saying something nice. We know this because her mom thanks her.
5. You find out that Darcy's mom has three hands.
6. In our world, people only have two hands, so the story cannot be realistic fiction.
7. The word *all* foreshadows that she might have more than two hands. If she had two hands, she probably would say, "Both of my hands are full."

"Biscuit Drop" (pages 20–23)
Summary: A mountain climber named Bates tested biscuits so he could find the right ones for an expedition to K2.

Vocabulary: hardy = "tough, doesn't break easily"; resistant = "strong, can keep something away"; expedition = "journey, trip"; route = "way, path, trail"

1. He threw them out of a second-floor window and left them in the rain overnight.
2. hardy and water-resistant; Bates tested them to see if they would crack and if they would get soggy, and his job was getting the food.
3. *Possible reasons:* It is "easier to climb," "not as steep," "not as hard to get to the top," and has a "well-worn route to the summit."
4. The top should be circled. The story uses *summit* and *top* interchangeably. The top of K2 is in the Death Zone. There is not enough oxygen.
5. 1, 2, and 5 should be filled in. The other two paragraphs are mainly about K2 and Everest, and how K2 is harder to climb.
6. We find out in the last paragraph.

"Animal Facts" (pages 24–27)
Summary: Tortoise thinks she can stop Rabbit from boasting by asking hard riddles. Rabbit answers all the riddles and then asks Tortoise a riddle.

Vocabulary: sneered = "smiled or spoke in a mean way"; jeered = "spoke or teased in a mean way"; homonym = "words that sound the same but have different meanings"

1. Tortoise. She doesn't boast, sneer, or jeer. She gives Rabbit a compliment.
2. What color socks does Bear wear?; You have to know that *bear* and *bare* are homonyms and that when your feet are bare, you are not wearing socks.
3. She's saying they are really easy; "They aren't hard questions at all."
4. She would compliment Rabbit.
5. nonfiction, because facts are true; right away, because rabbits can't boast
7. B; if you are weak, you are not strong (*weak* and *week* are homonyms)

"Edward Lear" (pages 28–31)
Summary: Edward Lear is a poet who wrote nonsense poems. One poem was about bird nests in a beard. Lear was ashamed because he had seizures.

1. Birds don't make nests in men's beards.
2. "Two Owls and a Hen, Four Larks and a Wren"; 8 total
3. He would feel ashamed and blame himself; no, because it wasn't his fault.
4. Yes, because he imagined things like birds making nests in beards.
5. paragraphs 3, 4, and 5; his life with his sister, and his seizures
6. It has five lines. In lines 1, 2, and 5, the words *beard*, *feared*, and *beard* all rhyme. In lines 3 and 4, the words *hen* and *wren* rhyme.

"Horribly Sick" (pages 32–35)
Summary: Mrs. Danza thinks Carlos is sick, because he is reading instead of playing video games or watching TV.

Vocabulary: b. respond = "react"; c. chatter = "talk"; d. symptoms = "signs"

1. playing video games or watching TV; because all the other children do it
2. largest marsupials in world, can swim, can't walk backward, hop on two legs, walk slowly on four, can jump three times their height, babies called joeys
3. a. mammals; b. Answers may vary. Human mothers don't carry their babies in pouches; c. Answers may vary. You can walk backwards.
4. He doesn't react at all. He is too interested in the book he is reading.
5. You find out that Carlos was reading and wasn't horribly sick.
   You find out that his mother doesn't understand why reading is so important.
6. No, because the surprise is that he was reading, not what he was reading about.
7. Mrs. Danza took the book Carlos was reading from his hands.

"Crocodile Tears" (pages 36–39)
Summary: Crocodiles cry when they eat, but not because they're sad. Their jaws are strong for biting down. People who shed crocodile tears are pretending to be sad.

Vocabulary: a. The crocodile consumes or eats its prey; b. The story calls the crocodile "the reptile"; c. The story says "crocodiles don't have emotions like people."

1. A crocodile has small and weak muscles for opening its mouth.
2. Tears clean their eyes, get rid of extra salt, and keep their eyes from drying out.
3. Casey is crying fake tears. "Someone may pretend to be sad or upset."

Answer Key

4. The crocodile should be circled for all three. The story tells us that crocodiles "have the strongest bite of any animal."
6. It is nonfiction, because it gives facts about crocodiles. "People can cry crocodile tears"; if one didn't know about the expression, it sounds impossible.

"Magic Trick" (pages 40–43)
Summary: Ravi wants some of Brandon's cookies, so he tricks Brandon by saying he will do a magic trick. The trick works, and Ravi eats all the cookies.
Vocabulary: entire = "whole, all"; mystified = "puzzled"; perform = "do something, act"; vanished = "disappeared"

1. Brandon had to take the hat off the plate.
2. a. "19" and "one less than twenty"; b. Answers will vary.
3. a. He is boasting and showing off; b. He is showing off that he made the cookies disappear and that he didn't touch the hat.
4. No, because all he did was trick Brandon into taking the hat off the plate.
5. Step 2. Put cookies on plate; Step 3. Cover cookies with hat; Step 4. Say you will eat all the cookies without touching the hat; Step 5. Say "Ta-Da!" and that all the cookies are gone; Step 6. When someone takes off the hat to check, you eat the cookies!
6. You would think Brandon will eat them, because it says he isn't going to share.

"Alive and Dead" (pages 44–47)
Summary: This story is all about hair. It tells about hair parts, hair color, and why our hair turns gray as we age.
Vocabulary:

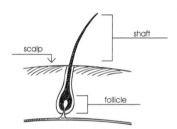

1. The story says hair *cannot* grow on lips, palms of hands, or soles of feet.
2. The shaft has no living part.
3. The cells that make melanin had begun to die.
4. The hair should be colored red. Hair color determines the number of hair follicles. Redheads have about 90,000.
5. In paragraphs 1 and 2, the questions are at the end. In 3 and 5, they are at the beginning.

"A Bare Escape" (pages 48–51)
Summary: Everyone thinks Andrea and Danielle will win the race, but Ann wins. She ran fast because she saw a bear and was running for her life.
Vocabulary: course = "path, track"; loop = "circle"; stunned = "amazed, speechless, in disbelief"; vicinity = "area close by"

1. They were surprised and assumed she had cheated. She usually came in last.
2. She bent over, panting. Phrases like "streaks of sweat ran down her face" and "gasping for breath" tell you that she was running fast.
3. They were very close. The width of a hair is very small.
4. Accept responses that follow the directions given.
5. Everyone has to go inside. A bear has escaped from the zoo and is in the vicinity.
6. There are not usually wild bears in parks, and Ann usually lost races.
7. Adrenaline helped Ann go faster than Andrea and Danielle.

"The Ins and Outs of Doors" (pages 52–55)
Summary: The writer thinks learning how to read is a waste of time. After she has trouble with doors because she can't read the words on them, she changes her mind.
Vocabulary: Students should shade in the set of doors on the left.

a. It said the doors were right next to each other.
b. The writer was looking for a different door. The story says that the door she found wasn't close to any other door.

1. She tried to go out the door that said ENTER.
2. Her opinion is that reading is a waste of time. "Then two things happened that caused me to alter my opinion."
3. The person feels the opposite. The writer's opinion about reading is the opposite from what it was at the beginning.
4. If you can read, you will know which doors to enter and exit.
5. The author would tell you that learning how to read is very important.

"Shooting Fish" (pages 56–59)
Summary: Migrating salmon are blocked by dams. Fish cannons can help them get to their spawning grounds.
Vocabulary: spawning ground = "where eggs are laid"; exhausted = "tired, all your energy is used up"; transport = "carry, send, bring to another place"

1. They provide water for crops, help make electricity, and help stop flooding.
2. Stage 2: Young salmon swim to ocean; Stage 3: Salmon return to spawning ground; Stage 4: Adult salmon lay eggs.
3. Yes, because 10 feet is deeper than a few feet of water, and it can land safely in a few feet of water. "A few" means two or three, which is less than 10.
4. The salmon cannon is better, because then the salmon are only out of the water "five to ten seconds." This keeps them safe.
5. Salmon need to get past dams and barriers in order to complete their migration.
6. The three solutions given are fish ladders, trapping and carrying, and using a fish cannon. The author thinks the fish cannon is best.

"Carrie the Carrier" (pages 60–63)
Summary: Carrie is a dog that picks up everything and carries it away. Trang likes her because Carrie picks up dolls. No one else does because of what else she picks up.

1. They thought she didn't know the difference between a doll, a slipper, a phone, and a backpack.
2. She does not want to give two cents to Mr. Dang. She wants to add to what he said about Carrie picking up anything. You know this because Mrs. Dang never gives Mr. Dang any money; instead, she tells how Carrie picked up her phone.
3. She grabbed the wrong basket and didn't get the kittens. It is difficult to think clearly when there is lots of noise, you're in a rush, and you're feeling scared.
4. Ellen's three kittens are in the basket. We know this because we are told that "three little whiskered faces" are poking out of the basket.
5. Carrie saves some kittens by carrying their basket out of a neighbor's smoke-filled apartment.
6. Most likely not. By saving the kittens, Carrie showed she could be very useful.
7. Mr. Dang: "She's as useful as a barrel with a hole in it"; Mrs. Dang: "She's a real menace."; Viet: "I think we should find her a new home."

Answer Key

"Never Growing Old" (pages 64–67)

Summary: Carroll Spinney plays Big Bird, a character on *Sesame Street*. Information is given about Big Bird and how the puppeteer does his job.

Vocabulary: b. *misname* means "to not name correctly"; c. *miscount* means "to not count correctly"; d. *mislead* means "to take in the wrong direction, not lead correctly"; e. *misbehave* means "not act or behave correctly"; f. *misuse* means "to not use correctly"; g. *misfortune* means "to not have good luck"

1. He grew younger. He used to be an adults, but is now 6 years old.
2. "No" should be circled. "He never grows older."
3. Spinney's head is in Big Bird's neck. His right hand is holding up Big Bird's head.
4. No, because Oscar also changed by turning from orange to green.
5. You are asked to try a hard task, which is to hold up four pounds with your right hand for a long time.

"Always First" (pages 68–71)

Summary: An older brother always goes first, saying, "Age before beauty." The sister knows it isn't fair.

Vocabulary: *exhibit* = "display, show"; *polite* = "nice, well mannered"; *firm* = "not wobbly or shaking"

1. Sam got the last carrots, and he had finished feeding them before Laura could ask him to share.
2. There is a chance, because she was told the zoo was closing ("The zoo is now closing.") when she tried to buy a giraffe treat.
3. One's age is more important than how one looks; the older lady should go first because age comes before looks.
4. No, she won't. Sam will be two years older, too. He will always be older.
5. Laura gives a speech about taking turns. Sam has to do more work now because he is older.
6. Grown-ups smile. His grandfather lets him pick which exhibit to see first, or he gets to feed the giraffes first; he is given more work because he is older.
7. The illustration shows that the brother is unhappy (frowning) and the sister is happy (smiling) at the news that he will be doing more work around the house.

"Sportsmanship" (pages 72–75)

Summary: Landy was in an important race. His spikes hit a runner who had fallen. He stopped running to make sure the runner was okay. He still won the race.

Vocabulary: *capable* = "able to do something"; *record* = "the best or highest score"; *clipped* = "to hit with a slight blow"; *spikes* = "sharp pieces of metal"

1. He had accidentally spiked another runner, and he wanted to make sure that person was okay.
2. "The spikes helped stop the runners from slipping."
3. a. It means "less than four minutes." The story is about both Bannister and Landy running miles in times less than four minutes; b. A subway would go below the ground, because *sub* means "below."
4. Landy held it longer. Bannister's record lasted 46 days, while Landy's lasted over three years. (Challenge: He broke the record in June. We know that Bannister set the record on May 6, and Landy broke it 46 days later.)
5. Information is given about Roger Bannister and how he was the first to break the four-minute mile.

"On the Leash" (pages 76–79)

Summary: The narrator tells you why pets should be on leashes and what happens when his pet is not on the leash. At the end, you find out the narrator is a dog.

Vocabulary: b. "is not" (The story says the leash was taut and wasn't sagging or drooping.); c. "is" (The story says the boy's pace was too slow for the dog.); d. "is" (The story says the dog releases heat to cool down.)

1. "makes a lot of noise."; he probably barks, because he is a dog.
2. safer, less likely to get hurt, less likely to get lost, less likely to get in fights
3. He was going really slow. The narrator had to pull on the leash to get him to go faster.
4. Students should draw a slide. The story describes the pet climbing up a high, steep ladder and then sliding down a steep metal hill.
5. You learn that the narrator is a dog. He tells you that like other dogs, he cools down by panting.

"Surviving the Fire" (pages 80–83)

Summary: Scientists put trackers on echidnas to find out how they survived fires. The echidnas go into a state called torpor in which they barely use any energy.

Vocabulary: *researcher* = "one who studies something, a scientist"; *roaming* = "moving about"; *snouts* = "noses"; *torpor* = "state where everything is slowed down"

1. They put trackers on them.
2. It might not be able to find enough food.
3. *Possible answers:* blackened areas have become green; seeds have sprouted; plants have grown; insects have hatched out of eggs.
4. "Most mammals give birth to live young. Echidnas don't. They lay eggs."
5. Scientists wanted study what fires do to plants and animals, so they lit a fire. After the fire, they saw strange spiny animals sticking their noses in ashes.
6. nonfiction; a. It tells about scientists who studied how real animals called echidnas survived fires. It is full of facts; b. Most mammals don't lay eggs, and if an animal doesn't move for four days, it most likely isn't alive.
7. It gets cold at night, and it's hard to find food. It takes energy to keep warm. By going into torpor, you save energy. You can wait out the cold and the night.

"Cat for Dessert" (pages 84–87)

Summary: Jane's dad is angry at her favorite uncle's cat. Jane's uncle makes everyone think they are having the cat for dessert. He is only teasing.

1. He laughs and tells him, "Don't ever change" when he sees the cat is a cake.
2. frosted with brown icing, gum drops for eyes, black licorice for whiskers
3. He said, "We're having the cat for dessert. I told you I'd make good use of it."
4. He had the beginning of an idea. He has the gleam in his eye when he says, "I'll put the cat to good use." That's when he first thinks of the joke.
5. He baked two cakes in two round cake pans. One cake was the body. He cut a tail and two ears out of the second cake. The rest of the cake was the head.

Meeting Standards

The lessons and activities included in *Close Reading with Text-Dependent Questions* meet the following Common Core State Standards for grade 2. (©Copyright 2010. National Governors Association Center for Best Practices and Council of Chief State School Officers. All rights reserved.)

The code for each standard covered in this resource is listed in the table below and on page 96. The codes are listed in boldface, and the unit numbers of the activities that meet that standard are listed in regular type. For more information about the Common Core State Standards and for a full listing of the descriptions associated with each code, go to http://www.corestandards.org/ or visit http://www.teachercreated.com/standards/.

Here is an example of an English Language Arts (ELA) code and how to read it:

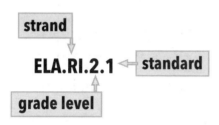

ELA Strands
- **L** = Language
- **W** = Writing
- **RI** = Reading: Informational Text
- **RL** = Reading: Literature
- **RF** = Reading: Foundation Skills
- **SL** = Speaking and Listening

Strand Reading: Informational Text **Substrand** Key Ideas and Details
- **ELA.RI.2.1:** Units 1–22
- **ELA.RI.2.2:** Units 1–22
- **ELA.RI.2.3:** Units 2, 4, 8, 10, 13, 15, 17, 19, 22

Strand Reading: Informational Text **Substrand** Craft and Structure
- **ELA.RI.2.4:** Units 1–22
- **ELA.RI.2.5:** Units 1–22
- **ELA.RI.2.6:** Units 1–22

Strand Reading: Informational Text **Substrand** Integration of Knowledge and Ideas
- **ELA.RI.2.8:** Units 1–22

Strand Reading: Informational Text **Substrand** Range of Reading and Level of Text Complexity
- **ELA.RI.2.7:** Units 17
- **ELA.RI.2.10:** Units 1–22

Strand Reading: Literature **Substrand** Key Ideas and Details
- **ELA.RL.2.1:** Units 1, 3, 5–7, 9, 11, 14, 16, 18, 20–21
- **ELA.RL.2.2:** Units 1, 3, 5–7, 9, 11, 14, 16, 18, 20–21
- **ELA.RL.2.3:** Units 1, 3, 5–7, 9, 11, 14, 16, 18, 20–21

Strand Reading: Literature **Substrand** Craft and Structure
- **ELA.RL.2.4:** Units 1, 3, 5–7, 9, 11, 14, 16, 18, 20–21
- **ELA.RL.2.5:** Units 1, 3, 5–7, 9, 11, 14, 16, 18, 20–21
- **ELA.RL.2.6:** Units 1, 3, 5, 7, 9, 14, 16, 18, 20–21

Meeting Standards

Strand Reading: Literature
ELA.RL.2.7: Units 1, 3, 5-7, 9, 11, 14, 16-18, 20-21
Substrand Integration of Knowledge and Ideas

Strand Reading: Literature
ELA.RL.2.10: Units 1, 3, 5-7, 9, 11, 14, 16, 18, 20-21
Substrand Range of Reading and Level of Text Complexity

+ +

Strand Reading: Foundational Skills
ELA.RF.2.3: Units 1-22
Substrand Phonics and Word Recognition

Strand Reading: Foundational Skills
ELA.RF.2.4: Units 1-22
Substrand Fluency

+ +

Strand Speaking and Listening
ELA.SL.2.1: Units 1-22
ELA.SL.2.2: Units 21-22
ELA.SL.2.3: Units 21-22
Substrand Comprehension and Collaboration

Strand Speaking and Listening
ELA.SL.2.4: Units 2, 6-8, 14, 21-22
ELA.SL.2.6: Units 1-9, 11-14, 16-19, 21-22
Substrand Presentation of Knowledge and Ideas

+ +

Strand Writing
ELA.W.2.1: Units 1-20
ELA.W.2.2: Units 1-20
ELA.W.2.3: Units 3, 7, 9-10, 12, 17-18, 20
Substrand Text Types and Purposes

Strand Writing
ELA.W.2.8: Units 1-22
Substrand Research to Build and Present Knowledge

+ +

Strand Language
ELA.L.2.1: Units 1-22
ELA.L.2.2: Units 1-22
Substrand Conventions of Standard English

Strand Language
ELA.L.2.3: Units 1-22
Substrand Knowledge of Language

Strand Language
ELA.L.2.4: Units 1-22
ELA.L.2.5: Units 1-22
ELA.L.2.6: Units 1-22
Substrand Vocabulary Acquisition and Use